─THE **WAY** OF THE─
SEAL

JOURNAL

A Step-by-Step Guide to
Thinking Like an Elite Warrior

A COMPANION TO THE
NATIONAL BESTSELLER

MARK DIVINE
Commander, U.S. Navy SEALs (Retired)

WITH ALLYSON EDELHERTZ MACHATE

Reader's
Digest

New York / Montreal

A READER'S DIGEST BOOK

Copyright © 2020 Mark Divine
All rights reserved. Unauthorized reproduction, in any manner, is prohibited.
Reader's Digest is a registered trademark of Trusted Media Brands, Inc.

ISBN 978-1-62145-479-3

We are committed to both the quality of our products and the service we provide
to our customers. We value your comments, so please feel free to contact us.

Reader's Digest Adult Trade Publishing
44 South Broadway
White Plains, NY 10601

For more Reader's Digest products and information, visit our website:
www.rd.com (in the United States)
www.readersdigest.ca (in Canada)

Printed in China

10 9 8 7 6 5 4 3 2 1

Contents

A Note to the Reader

Personal transformation books are one of the most popular types of nonfiction out there. But there's a big difference between reading such a book and working such a book.

Since the first edition of *The Way of the SEAL* was published in 2013, I have received unbelievable feedback from readers on the power of the principles and the changes they've initiated in so many lives. I've taught the tools and principles in a number of different settings since the book's first publication as well, and I've had dozens of people show me their copy of the book, all dog-eared, text highlighted, and notes in the margins. Additionally, the principles have found their way into corporate teams, high school and university courses on leadership and entrepreneurship, military special ops training, prisons, and the post-traumatic stress recovery program of the Courage Foundation.

If you've read the original book, then you know constant change is a given and innovation is essential. We published an updated and expanded edition of *The Way of the SEAL* in 2018 to address shifting conditions in the leadership space and in the world. Now, I'm really excited to present this companion journal as a new way to engage with the material to up your WOS training and to lead and succeed at an uncommon level.

If you haven't read *The Way of the SEAL* yet, I highly recommend you do so before trying to work through the following exercises. The instructional context of the exercises, as well as my personal stories and those of others who have deployed the principles, are an important part of the learning process. The book and this workbook together make a powerful team designed to guide and support you on your journey to thinking like an elite warrior.

Before getting into the exercises, it will be useful to review their guiding principles. Then you can begin working to develop your Way of the SEAL (WOS) mind-set and start enjoying the benefits of frogman-style leadership at both the individual and team levels.

Leadership in an Accelerating World

The business world is as volatile, uncertain, complex, and ambiguous (VUCA) as a SEAL battlefield, so organizational leaders need to develop a SEAL-like leadership mind-set to stay competitive and succeed. This means they also need to become comfortable with discomfort and be prepared for the unexpected at all times.

Establish Your Set Point

You will need to establish your set point before you set off into VUCA territory. The set point places you firmly on your internal map with greater awareness of the thoughts and decisions that got you where you are today. You will commit to closing gaps in your own leadership development through incremental change, which results from a daily practice of self-mastery in service to others.

Develop Front-Sight Focus

Maintaining a radical attention on the right things while on the attack is the only way to see massive mission success. To get front-sight focused, you will learn to win in your mind before stepping foot into battle. With WOS mental tools, you will be able to see your choices more clearly and knock out high-value targets in quick succession.

Bulletproof Your Mission

Bulletproofing your mission hardens your targets, team, and mission plan against enemy fire (otherwise known as "shit going sideways"). Selecting the right targets from the start is key to success. Communicating the mission relentlessly so that each team member can envision their part allows for total alignment around a shared vision, leading to domination of the battlefield.

Do Today What Others Won't

This principle will inspire you to train harder than others and to be confident that you are capable of twenty times more than you think.

As you step into the arena—whether it be an athletic competition, a business negotiation, or even your work as a parent—you will embrace the suck and truly love the exponential growth that your uncommon effort brings.

Forge Mental Toughness

Emotions can torpedo even the smartest leader's progress, so developing emotional resilience and getting control of your reactionary mind are the next crucial skills. Mental toughness requires that you harness your mental focusing power and get control over raw emotions that cause you to react in ways that hurt you or others. You will learn to transform negative thoughts and emotions into positive motivation and build the resiliency to stay in the fight.

Break Things

No plan survives contact with a VUCA environment, so the WOS is to plan for failure, then fail your way to success as fast as possible. When you systematize trial and error while leveraging responsive, fast-twitch planning tools, you can break things the smart way—like a SEAL!—to capitalize on new opportunities as quickly as they arise.

Build Your Intuition

Intuition is the secret weapon of the WOS leader, but it can be challenging to hear your inner voice over the noise of a lifetime of negative experiences and destructive mental programming. As you reconnect with your innate wisdom through sensory development and meditation practices, you will uncover your background of obviousness (BOO) and learn to prevent it from torpedoing your best laid plans. Clearing up your BOO will be the most challenging aspect of being a WOS leader.

Think Offense, All the Time

Leading in an accelerating world can't be a defensive act; instead you will learn to think offensively and with unwavering confidence. The threats are everywhere. The WOS leader can spot them and will best be able to avoid them rather than having to fight a way through.

When you cultivate an offensive mind-set, you'll keep things fresh, always learning and growing and keeping your competitors off balance.

Training in the Way of the SEAL

The principles outlined in the book are great for reflection, but the real work is in the exercises and daily practices. You will not be able to master them in a moment—so employ a "slow is smooth, smooth is fast" approach. Changing the way you approach training for yourself and with your team is part of your WOS transformation and will ensure your success.

The Secrets of Elite Teams

Your journey as a leader is not a solo act: Elite leaders need an elite team at their backs to help execute the mission. You will learn how to foster a "together, we grow" mind-set where each teammate is challenging and supporting the others to develop new capacities and build new skills. You will stand out with a communication strategy of brutal honesty, where you will brief and debrief every important initiative for constant improvement. The team will work as a "team of teams" with a structure that demonstrates high degrees of integrity, but almost unlimited flexibility.

When everyone takes ownership of the mission and team's success, you will create unbeatable momentum.

Good luck with your training! If you need help in any way, I hope you'll reach out to me at info@unbeatablemind.com.

—Mark Divine
Encinitas, California, 2019

LEADERSHIP IN AN ACCELERATING WORLD

- The business world looks like a SEAL's VUCA battlefield, so it is necessary for business and other organizational leaders to develop a SEAL-like leadership mind-set, becoming comfortable with discomfort and preparing for the unexpected.

- Volatility is surfed with a strong vision and radical focus on the mission. Teammates must be empowered to seek clarity of intent and take actions to move toward mission success regardless of the turbulence.

- Uncertainty can be overcome with a deeper understanding of the thought patterns that underlie the behavior of key players in the marketplace or battleground, and these patterns are shared by all human beings as part of our neurological makeup. Becoming aware of our own biases and developing a practice of introspection and observation so we can spot them in others are therefore key skills for leaders.

- Complexity is navigated by becoming adept at perspective taking on all the stakeholders in the environment, then regrouping to see the bigger picture, reframing for a higher level and simpler solution, and recharging the mission focus.

- Ambiguity is obliterated with agile, fast-twitch iteration planning, and failing forward fast toward your objective.

Simplifying Complexity

Here are some good questions to get us "back to simple" when stuck in complexity:

- Why are we, as a team, undertaking this mission? What is our vision for victory and why is this important?

_____

_____

_____

_____

- Is each teammate in sync with this vision?

_____

_____

_____

_____

- If not, why? What individual perspectives are causing a disconnect?

_____

_____

_____

_____

- Can we reframe the vision to be inclusive of our diverse perspectives?

_____

_____

_____

_____

- What is the most viable plan for the mission? Why?

_____

_____

_____

_____

- Which main target should we focus on first? Why? What about after that? Why?

_____

_____

_____

_____

- Would a complete stranger find our plan simple enough to execute?

_____

_____

_____

_____

- What do we do if/when A, B, or C happens on the way to the target?

_____

_____

_____

_____

REFLECTIONS AND INSIGHTS _____

_____

_____

_____

_____

_____

_____

_____

_____

_____

_____

_____

_____

_____

_____

_____

_____

_____

_____

_____

_____

_____

_____

_____

_____

_____

_____

_____

_____

_____

_____

_____

_____

_____

_____

_____

_____

_____

_____

_____

_____

_____

_____

_____

_____

_____

_____

_____

_____

_____

_____

_____

_____

_____

_____

_____

_____

_____

_____

_____

ESTABLISH YOUR SET POINT

- A set point is an awareness of where you are now in terms of your skills, knowledge, and values and the thoughts and decisions that got you here. To evolve into an elite operator, you must be willing to commit to closing gaps you may see in your own leadership development through incremental change, which results from a daily practice of self-mastery in service to others.

- Knowing where you stand in life requires a deep reflection on what principles you believe in and are willing to live by, so that your actions reflect your stand. This takes courage and discipline.

- Finding your purpose in life, that essence of what your inner voice tells you is your reason for being on this planet, will allow you to always answer the question "why" and inform what you will do when things get tough.

- To move forward and accelerate your vertical development using the WOS principles, you must embrace risk, be willing to lose things you once valued but that don't serve you any longer, and learn to get comfortable with failure.

THE WAY OF THE SEAL (WOS) ASSESSMENT

This multipart exercise begins the journey of self-discovery with a relaxation and contemplation exercise. As you ponder the questions, pay close attention to any images and feelings that arise—these raw initial impressions come from your subconscious mind, as yet unfiltered, unanalyzed, and uncategorized. These are the clearest signs pointing to your purpose. Try not to judge what comes up, even (or especially!) if the message seems scary.

Part 1: Build Your Stand

Your stand answers the question "What would I do?" First, find a comfortable place to sit with your journal, perhaps a chair or on the floor with your back against a wall. Make sure your spine is straight. Close your eyes and breathe with deep abdominal breaths for at least five minutes. While breathing, just relax deeply.

After at least five minutes of deep breathing, open your eyes and contemplate the questions below. Write your answers quickly, paying attention to the images and feelings that come up.

- What would I do if I knew I only had one year to live?

_____

_____

_____

_____

- What would I do if a natural disaster or terrorist event struck my town?

_____

_____

_____

_____

_____

• What would I do if a friend asked me to help him move but I really wanted to go see a movie that night?

_____

_____

_____

_____

_____

_____

_____

• What would I do if I found out my favorite brand had been exploiting workers and participating in environmentally destructive practices?

_____

_____

_____

_____

_____

_____

_____

• What would I do if I won the lottery?

_____

_____

_____

_____

_____

_____

- What would I do if someone decided to fight me for no good reason?

_____

_____

_____

_____

_____

_____

_____

- What would I do if an opportunity for an inside deal came my way with little chance of anyone finding out?

_____

_____

_____

_____

_____

_____

_____

- What would I do if my team were bashing a teammate behind his back in my presence?

_____

_____

_____

_____

_____

_____

_____

Now think about what your answers say about your character. For instance, my answer to the last question is "I'd keep my mouth shut and leave, if possible." For my stand, this translates into "I respect people's right to have an opinion, but I will not engage in negative talk or gossip." You'll think of your own questions based on what is important to you as you get rolling—remember this is your stand, not mine. Try to come up with six to ten statements that feel really powerful and right for you.

_____

_____

_____

_____

_____

_____

_____

_____

_____

_____

_____

_____

_____

_____

_____

_____

_____

_____

_____

_____

Part 2: Define Your Values

The second part of this is to clarify your values so you can become the kind of person who can stand his or her ground every day. Values answer the question "What do I want more of or less of in my life?"

Write down those things you would like to move toward and a few things you would like to move away from. To guide you, here are my values for living a good life, phrased according to what I want to be more like (you can also just list the base values themselves, for example, health and positivity, love and passion, etc.):

- healthy and positive
- loving and passionate
- wise and authentic
- grateful and truthful
- playful and fun
- learning and growing
- bold and decisive
- contributing to others

Examples of "less of" values from my list include:

- negative and judgmental
- attached and cluttered
- selfish

More of

_____

_____

_____

_____

_____

_____

Less of

_____

_____

_____

_____

_____

_____

_____

Part 3: Discover Your Passion

Now let's do some fun fantasizing. The reason you want to clarify what you're passionate about is so you can put energy toward doing more of it, which will help keep you motivated toward positive change! Your passions are the answer to "Who am I at my deepest level?" Chances are, your passions point the way toward your purpose, the end goal of this exercise. Start by asking yourself the questions below. Ask them one at a time and write down whatever comes to you. Remember: Pay attention to your first impressions and try not to judge.

1. What books, movies, art, or music gets you pumped?

_____

_____

_____

_____

_____

2. Who inspires you and why?

_____

_____

_____

_____

_____

3. What characteristics of yours make you feel great about yourself?

_____

_____

_____

_____

_____

4. What activities would you do if you had more time and no barriers?

_____

_____

_____

_____

_____

5. What is meaningful to you about these activities?

_____

_____

_____

_____

_____

6. What benefit to others would these activities or characteristics provide?

_____

_____

_____

_____

_____

7. Could you change the world, making it even a tiny bit better, by focusing more on these?

_____

_____

_____

_____

_____

8. What would it take to get you to step into the arena of even just one of these activities?

_____

_____

_____

_____

As with writing your stand, if you find your answers skewing negatively—for example, if you see no benefit to others in your activities or don't see yourself effecting change in the world in even a small way—you've stumbled upon an opportunity for deep reflection. What's really motivating you in life?

Part 4: Uncover Your Purpose

This final step is often the most difficult for my trainees. For maximum effect, I encourage you to investigate a "being" purpose. For instance, my first articulated purpose was to be a warrior leader and to master myself so that I could fulfill that purpose to the best of my ability. Along the way to fulfilling that purpose, I naturally included some goals that focused on external achievements, such as earning the Navy SEAL Trident (representing graduation from the arduous two-year training pipeline), leading a SEAL platoon, and becoming an expert trainer. However, these weren't my primary focuses. My purpose centered on a concept of self-transformation, of becoming something at the character level, not on the mere acquisition of a title or position.

I did not choose as my purpose "to become a SEAL officer, attaining the rank of admiral." Even though it technically includes "being" something, this kind of purpose puts your focus only on the label, not the contents within.

Armed with your new self-awareness from Parts 1 to 3, contemplate all the possibilities that look, feel, or sound as if they're in line with your passion, values, and stand.

Take time now to write a few sentences or paragraphs defining your purpose in life.

_____

_____

_____

_____

_____

_____

_____

_____

_____

_____

_____

_____

_____

_____

_____

_____

_____

_____

_____

_____

Come back to it often and refine it as the insights roll in. I like to check in with my purpose daily and often find myself changing a proposed action I had planned or even a word in my statement. All of these—your stand, values, passion, and even your purpose—are subject to grow and change as you do.

ENVISION YOUR "FUTURE ME"

When you're satisfied with the results from the previous assessments, it's time to develop an internal representation of you at your absolute finest as a human, designed around fulfilling your purpose, living with passion and in alignment with your values, all while standing your ground. Doing so will reinforce your self-discovery process and give you a stimulating, motivating vision to remind you why you're doing all this work! It'll also start to build your visualization muscles.

Even though you may not feel or look the part now, you must envision yourself in your ideal state, activating your personal power and living in alignment with your stand and purpose. I learned in the SEALs that there's no such thing as perfection, only perfect effort. Through practicing a "perfect" version of ourselves mentally, we'll slowly become that person in real life.

Step 1: Find a comfortable place to sit—I encourage you to use the same space you used for your WOS Assessment, a place that can become your "sit space" or meditation room. Close your eyes and breathe with deep abdominal breaths for at least five minutes. While breathing, just relax. After at least five minutes of deep breathing, begin the visualization as described below.

Step 2: In your mind's eye, conjure up an image of you in your ideal state three months from now. See yourself as having already accomplished your intermediate goals, in perfect health, and fully embodying the character traits that represent your stand, values, and purpose. As this image becomes clear, add color, sound, emotions, and movement to it, as if you were watching yourself in a movie. This process should take only a couple minutes.

Step 3: Now fast-forward and repeat the imagery, but from the point of view of one year out. Then, if you desire, take it out three years and repeat.

Step 4: When you are satisfied with your "Future Me" visions, collapse them all to the present moment and see yourself now as that person. See yourself as someone who has already earned your personal Trident. Own it and breathe into that vision. When you are done, simply open your eyes and carry on with your day, leaving your subconscious mind to do its part.

REFLECTIONS AND INSIGHTS _____

_____

_____

_____

_____

_____

_____

_____

_____

_____

_____

_____

_____

_____

_____

_____

_____

_____

_____

_____

DEVELOP FRONT-SIGHT FOCUS

- Front-sight focus is a radical focus on the mission and the targets that will get you to mission success—with the simplest, most effective plan.

- To get front-sight focused, the leader must learn to win in his or her mind before embarking on the mission. This requires mental preparation in the form of embracing silence and learning to take control over the active, thinking, and judging mind.

- When the mind can focus clearly, the WOS leader creates a powerful internal image of what victory looks like and frequently revisits that image personally and with the team. This enables you to knock out the right, high-value targets in relatively quick succession and with confidence, ensuring high levels of success.

- Defining the mission for the team by clarifying both specific and implied intent, and aligning the team to that intent, will allow the team to head off potential distractions and remain front-sight focused.

- Removing unnecessary targets, mental and physical clutter, and any thoughts besides total mission focus will lead to success regardless of how challenging the mission or fast-moving the environment.

DEEP BREATHING CYCLES

In a quiet spot where you won't be disturbed, get comfortable and close your eyes. Slowly draw a breath through your nose, filling your lungs from the bottom up. As you do so, your diaphragm will press your stomach out. Now exhale, also through your nose, flattening your belly and chest as you do so. Continue for at least four cycles—by then the pattern should feel more comfortable, and you should feel relaxed and at ease. You can use deep breathing to calm yourself and clear your mind in any situation. Try it the next time you feel nervous or angry.

STILL WATER RUNS DEEP

Sitting in a chair or against the wall, ensure that your back is straight, your chin is slightly tucked, and you're comfortable. Now gently close your eyes and bring your awareness to your breathing. Go through five cycles of deep breathing as described earlier, visualizing your body calming down from head to toes. After this, release into a natural breathing pattern but maintain focus on your breath.

In your mind's eye, see yourself sitting at the bottom of a deep pond. Feel the serenity and silence as you look around and up at the clear, sparkling water of the surface. Any thoughts that arise are mere ripples. After a while, if you choose, you can let this vision dissolve and just focus on your breathing. Now, start counting each breath cycle. If, after two counts, you suddenly realize you've been thinking about a big project at work, no worries. Just let it float to the surface and dissolve, then start the count over. Your objective is to get to ten without any conscious thought. This is much more difficult than it sounds! Practice for five minutes at least once a day for thirty days. Once you feel you are well on your way to quieting your mind, you can blend this with other practices in this book.

FANTASIZING WITH PURPOSE

- **Step 1: "See" it.** You'll need to get clear about your desired outcome. We'll discuss how to plan your mission in the next chapter, but for now just focus on defining where you want to end up.

- **Step 2: Imagine it.** You must imagine the outcome as if you've already achieved it. Most people can fantasize; with envisioning, you're creating a purposeful fantasy. This step requires a baseline reference to ground it in reality: Establish a visual reference point (to make your fantasy more concrete) and insert yourself into the imagery. References can be actual experiences, still photographs, or moving images (like my use of the SEALs' *Be Someone Special* video).

- **Step 3: Practice it.** Play your imagined reality in your mind daily. I recommend you do it as part of a powerful Morning or Evening Ritual (found on pages 104–109). For maximum effectiveness, you must infuse your visualization with belief, expectation, and an intense desire to bring the visualized event to life.

QUESTION THE MISSION

To get clear on the implicit tasks your leaders are asking you to do (or what you're asking of yourself), you must ask deeper questions, such as:

- Why am I doing this? Is it aligned with our overall mission as a company/team?

_____

_____

_____

_____

_____

- Is there some higher-priority project that may take precedence and sidetrack me?

_____

_____

_____

_____

_____

• Who else, if anyone, is involved in getting this project done?

_____

_____

_____

_____

_____

• What exactly is expected of me and any others who may be involved?

_____

_____

_____

_____

_____

• How and when can I count on them to fulfill their commitments?

_____

_____

_____

_____

_____

• What other subtasks are required before I can fulfill what's expected of me?

_____

_____

_____

_____

_____

- What other tasks are required in order for me to accomplish this mission?

_____

_____

_____

_____

_____

WIN IN YOUR MIND

This exercise will help you build a mental defense against distractions; you must have a clear mind in order to effectively choose and pursue your targets and achieve mission success. Let's set the conditions for you to win in your mind so you can maintain front-sight focus and win in life.

Part 1: The Sentinel at the Gate

In this exercise, you'll set up a mental sentinel to witness what's going on inside your brain. This sentinel will observe and report on any negative or unnecessary thoughts (and there will be a lot of both!).

Find your quiet spot (ideally you'll choose one place where you can do all of your mental work). Sit in a chair, lie down, or sit in any position that allows you to keep your back straight comfortably without fidgeting. Begin this exercise with five minutes of deep breathing, your eyes closed. Mentally watch your breath.

Now, release your focus on the breath and just pay attention to what comes up in your mind. This is tricky, but you'll get the hang of it soon. The part of you that is noticing or witnessing your thoughts is your sentinel. If it helps, you can imagine a guard or soldier sitting at the control panel of your consciousness, scanning your input and output. When your sentinel notices that you're thinking of something, don't fight it—acknowledge it, let it go, and return to witnessing your thoughts. Are they positive or negative? Are they random or directed? This is important for what follows. You can repeat this part of the exercise several times before moving on to Part 2.

Part 2: DIRECT Your Mind

This is your express train to mental control. Now that you're developing the capacity to observe the inner workings of your mind, we want your sentinel to start directing your thought traffic. Return to your quiet spot. This time, as random thoughts bubble up, implement the DIRECT process below. When you feel comfortable with this powerful method, try to DIRECT your thoughts during the day, especially those destructive to your well-being and front-sight focus.

Detect. Your sentinel will detect any thoughts that slip into your mind. Though we'd like to believe our thoughts are under our control, guess again. Thoughts arise constantly, and many have no business being in our minds, nor do they have a positive purpose in our lives. Road rage, what goes through your mind when someone cuts you off in traffic, is a good example of an emotion-driven thought. This happens to the best of us, but every thought distracting your front-sight focus depletes your energy and must be dealt with.

Interdict. If your sentinel detects a negative or useless thought, interdict it with a simple command such as "Stop!" or "No!" When you tell yourself to stop thinking something, guess what? You'll stop . . . for a moment.

Redirect. Once you stop a negative thought, you have to redirect your mind to new, empowering thoughts. When another driver cuts you off, triggering thoughts of revenge, your sentinel detects and then interdicts with "Stop!" The redirect occurs with a short dialogue, such as "Too bad that guy's having a bad day, but I'm not going to let him ruin mine. I'm focusing on the positive now." Your mind will welcome the new, positive direction.

Energize. Solidify the new thought by getting your whole being to support it, entering a new physiological state that matches your mental shift. For example, conjure images of yourself looking strong, confident, and positive. Now, feel it! Sit up straight, break a big smile, and laugh. Breathe deeply and feel the strong, confident, and positive energy course through your body. No one can spoil your good mood!

Communicate. This step is an insurance policy: You must talk to yourself in a new way to override any lurking negativity and prevent new destructive thoughts from creeping in. In SEAL training, I used the mantra "Feeling good, looking good, ought to be in Hollywood!" to maintain my energy and focus in the grind. I have also used "Day by day, in every way, I am getting better and better."

Train. Your mind can be a powerful ally or a slothful fiend. Practice the DIRECT technique daily like you would exercise your body, and it will not only give you control in the moment but also train your mind to function at an elite level permanently.

BUILD YOUR MIND GYM

To develop your visualization skills and to give structure, focus, and momentum to your practice, we're going to build a gym in your mind, a special room where you will do your mental training. Eventually, visiting your mind gym will become a habit that will immediately center you and help you maintain front-sight focus, channeling all your willpower and energy toward whatever you seek to achieve. It's particularly useful as framework for your mental projections.

Find a comfortable position, close your eyes, and let the world begin to fade away. Take a few deep breaths to center yourself. Focus on the breath as it enters and leaves your body. In and out . . . in and out. Follow your breath to stillness. Bring your awareness to the here and now, and let all thoughts and worries of the day, all noisy distractions around you, just flow on through your mind without taking hold. Let it all go.

Now imagine yourself walking down a path. You are not in a hurry, but you see a set of stairs off to the right in the distance. You walk to the stairs and turn to look down. There are ten steps. You slowly walk down, taking a full breath with each step. Ten, nine, eight . . . When you reach the bottom, you see an archway. This is the door to your training area, where you will build your mind gym. You take another breath and step through the door.

You are now in your special training area. It may look familiar to you. Look around and behold the beautiful surroundings. Whatever shows up for you is okay—it may be a beach, a mountain, or a valley.

It may not even seem to be from this planet. In this place of yours, gravity has no effect, and you can do anything you want for your own good or the good of humanity. No one else can come into this place unless you invite them. This is where you will come to meditate, visualize, practice skills, and seek healing in the future. Now let's begin to construct your mind gym in this space.

The mind gym can look any way you want to imagine it. My mind gym is on a mountainside, has a wooden floor but no ceiling, a space to train in yoga and hand-to-hand combat, and a seated mat for meditating. It looks somewhat like a yoga studio or a martial arts dojo. Now build yours. Does it have windows, or is it open to the sky? Are the floors wood or carpeted? What colors or types of artwork decorate the walls? What equipment do you need? Leave one wall blank to use as a screen for mental projection work. Otherwise, fill this gym with whatever you might need to practice in your mind and whatever brings you a sense of peace. Today, this first visit, all you need to do is build the space.

When you're finished and satisfied with your work, express gratitude for this gift of a safe, pristine place to train. Now leave your mind gym and make your way back to the doorway. Look back and review your handiwork. When you're ready, turn and step through the door, and then climb the steps back up to your outer conscious self, one at a time. Each step up brings you closer to your normal, wide-awake state. When you reach the top, follow the path back out into the active world, slowly bringing awareness to each part of your body. You will feel alert and energized as you open your eyes to end the exercise.

KISS (Keep It Simple, Smarty)

Fewer distractions and undivided resources equal stronger front-sight focus and better results, so "keep it simple, smarty." This tool is taught everywhere from elementary schools to business retreats because it works! Here's the WOS application.

Step 1: Begin by decluttering your daily spaces, working your way from small (your desk) to big (your garage). You don't have to do it all at once—tackle just one corner a day.

Step 2: Next, analyze your unique offer as described on page 47 of *The Way of the SEAL (Updated and Expanded Edition)*, and start parsing your daily tasks to identify your key 20 percent. For one week, record everything you do in 30-minute blocks, from Facebook time and commuting to working, training, even sleeping. Go deeper and record how you're spending time within those blocks. For example, while at work, are you checking e-mail twice a day or every ten minutes? At the end of the week, analyze and chunk it down to get a picture of what you're really doing every day. Now that you know, you can weed out those actions or time-sucks that aren't serving you so you can focus on producing the results you want.

Step 3: Finally, it's time to clear out your internal junk by eliminating unwanted or otherwise distracting obligations, grudges, past grievances, negative beliefs, and unfinished emotional business. Anticipate and accept that there will be hard choices; seek to travel light internally and make a positive impact, otherwise treading softly on the world. This is the Way of the SEAL.

Following these three steps helps make simplicity a visceral experience. You can intellectualize something, but there's a certain point where you need to embody or experience a concept before you really understand it. That's why we start with clearing stuff out physically. If you faithfully perform all three steps, you can't help but get the power of KISS at a root level. And because KISS applies to everything you do, you'll be able to integrate the concept into all aspects of your life. Increasing your effectiveness by making things simpler is an unbeatable combination.

REFLECTIONS AND INSIGHTS _____

_____

_____

_____

_____

BULLETPROOF YOUR MISSION

- Bulletproofing your mission means to do everything possible to eliminate potential obstacles and harden your team and mission plan against enemy fire.

- Selecting the right targets—the highest-value ones that fit your vision, mission, and team's unique potential—is key to success. WOS leaders will learn to use the rapid planning FITS tool for this.

- Once the most viable targets are selected, the leader and elite team must evaluate all the options and select the simplest and most compelling one. The WOS leader will use the PROP tool for this.

- Communicating the mission plan by telling a story in which everyone can see their part allows the mission vision to be shared by the entire team. There won't be conflicting views on what success is or what the rules of engagement are.

- Elite teams will dirt-dive, or mentally rehearse, the overall mission and their team or individual roles once they have a clear vision of the entire op. This dirt-dive becomes standard operating procedure (SOP) for elite teams before they step off the ramp.

CREATE A BULLETPROOF MISSION PLAN

In this exercise, you will work through a mock mission plan related to either your business or personal life—for example, to launch a new product, service, or venue, or to lose weight.

Part 1: Select a Target That FITS

Use the FITS process (Fit, Importance, Timing, and Simplicity) to analyze your potential targets (which should all be SMART goals, as described in Principle 5), and narrow the choices to the most high-value targets so you can map out an effective mission plan. You can use the guidelines provided to evaluate a preselected target, or you can use a simple 1 to 5 ranking system for each category to help de-termine which target out of several is optimal. The latter approach would serve well as an opportunity analysis tool to rank new business or project possibilities.

- **Fit.** Does the target you're considering fit your team? Is it the best use of talent, time, and energy? What will it cost to engage this target, and does the return on investment (ROI) make it worth the effort?

_____

_____

_____

_____

_____

- **Importance.** How important is the target to your broader strategic mission? What effect will mission accomplishment have on you? On your competitors?

_____

_____

_____

_____

_____

- **Timing.** Is the timing right to go after this target? Are you too early or too late? Are you ready? Can you find and reach the target, and how is the competition going to respond when you reach it?

_____

_____

_____

_____

_____

- **Simplicity.** Is the target simple and clear? Is it something you can achieve without degrading your reputation, future capacities, or team cohesiveness?

_____

_____

_____

_____

_____

Part 2: PROP Up Your Actions

Armed with your selected high-value target(s), use the PROP system (Priorities, Realities, Options, and Path) to develop at least three courses of action and choose one clear path forward.

- **Priorities.** Of your high-value targets, determine and prioritize your top three or four for mission success. Are there any other priorities related to achieving your top high-value targets?

_____

_____

_____

_____

_____

- **Realities.** Get clear about the realities of your current situation and the influence these have on your targets and overall mission. How do these aspects affect your ability to satisfy your priorities?

_____

_____

_____

_____

_____

- **Options.** Based on your evaluation of your priorities and situation, develop and rank up to three options or courses of action for achieving your top high-value targets and, ultimately, your mission. Often you'll end up combining elements from two or all three options in the final plan. (Note: You can use a creativity-building exercise like the one below to help support this step.)

_____

_____

_____

_____

_____

- **Path.** Which course of action is the best fit? This is your path, along which you will develop your plan for hitting each target on the way to overall mission success.

_____

_____

_____

_____

_____

Part 3: SMACC Down Your Mission

Decide on an initial course of action from Part 2, and create the visual mosaic or "story" you will use to communicate the mission to others. You can frame your story with a process I call SMACC:

- **Situation.** What are the background circumstances leading to a need for action? Why is it that the target FITS the team right here and now? You must envision and research every detail so everyone can understand the backdrop to your mission.

_____

_____

_____

_____

_____

- **Mission.** What exactly is the mission? Write a statement using SMART terminology (Specific, Measurable, Achievable, Relevant, and Timely or Time-Bound—see Principle 5 for more on this). Make sure you include your targets and use words that conjure images in your audience's mind.

_____

_____

_____

_____

_____

- **Action.** What actions will your operating team perform? What about your administrative and logistical support teams? Actions are the meat and potatoes of your plan. No plan survives contact with the enemy—meaning that reality often requires adjustments—so make sure you include contingencies for when things go wrong.

_____

_____

_____

_____

_____

- **Command.** Who's in charge of what and when? This is important, since leadership roles will likely shift during the mission. Plan contingencies for this part as well.

_____

_____

_____

_____

_____

- **Communication.** How will teammates communicate with each other and to others? Who will communicate which messages in what timeframe using what methods?

_____

_____

_____

_____

_____

Use visual terms and avoid jargon; for example, say, "It'll be dark as heck" instead of "The illumination will be at 10 percent due to a waning moon." Use pictures and videos to tell your story. Have your team visualize completing the mission at each stage, and then rehearse it physically and/or mentally as appropriate to the mission.

THE IDEA LAB

Bulletproofing your mission against failure in part depends on ensuring you've chosen your targets wisely. Before you can use the tools in this chapter to assess your options, you need to become aware of what they are! This exercise is essentially a WOS approach to brainstorming that can be just as effective at the individual level as with a team. When you're considering your options for pursuing a target, for example, begin by putting on your "Morale Officer" hat and ensure you are in a positive, playful, and creative state of mind. In your journal, articulate your challenge clearly, drawing pictures if possible to tap into the powers of your subconscious.

Now, stop thinking. Sit in silence with your eyes closed, letting your mind settle. Visit your mind gym following the usual meditation as outlined on page 25. When you get there, you will use it as an idea lab by bringing your attention back to the challenge or question as you've articulated it and just watch the projection screen and wait for a response. You'll want to record whatever comes up, so to avoid interrupting your flow, consider having a mini-recorder or journal handy. It's important that you remember not to fall back on critical thinking about a solution; rather, let your mind remain clear and receptive to new insights. Record anything valuable that rises into your consciousness, whether it is a word, a fully formed thought, a feeling, or an image.

_____

_____

_____

_____

_____

_____

_____

_____

_____

_____

_____

_____

_____

_____

After five or ten minutes, transfer the innovative ideas onto sticky notes on a white board. Now, review your collection of notes and see what connections or further thoughts spring to mind. First impressions are typically closest to the mark, no matter how odd they may seem, so refrain from judging yours. Anything goes.

If you're doing this exercise with a team, the instructions are essentially the same. State the challenge out loud so everyone is on the same page, then have each participant visit their mind gym or just sit silently if they aren't familiar with the mind gym practice. Everyone should speak their ideas, images, and impressions out loud while one person records. Remember, anything goes, so no judging each other while you review the results.

_____

_____

_____

_____

_____

_____

_____

_____

_____

_____

_____

_____

_____

_____

_____

_____

_____

REFLECTIONS AND INSIGHTS _____

_____

_____

_____

_____

_____

_____

_____

_____

_____

_____

_____

_____

_____

_____

_____

_____

_____

_____

_____

_____

_____

_____

_____

_____

_____

DO TODAY WHAT OTHERS WON'T

- The creed "Do today what others won't, do tomorrow what others can't" should inspire you and your team to train harder than other people now so you can find success later amid challenges that would throw the less-prepared off track. This attitude is required of the WOS leader.

- You are capable of 20X more than you think at any given time. This is stored as latent, untapped potential. The WOS tools will unlock this potential, but it is up to you to go to the challenge to prove it to yourself.

- As you step into the arena of worthy challenges (by WOS standards), you will learn to embrace the suck of hard work and begin to thoroughly enjoy the growth that extraordinary effort brings.

- To fully embrace the suck, you will need to lean on the "Three Ds" of Discipline, Drive, and Determination. These will give you the freedom to choose your course of action, the internal positive motivation to stay focused, and the willpower to see the mission to fruition.

TRANSMUTING PAIN INTO POSITIVITY

As you tackle your next challenge, whether of the daily variety or a mighty effort, embrace the suck of the moment by shifting your focus to something positive, smiling, and even making yourself laugh. Take control of your story and use positive self-talk to reinforce your attitude adjustment. Connect the pain of the moment to your purpose and goals and know, deep inside, that you are traveling the upward spiral to success.

In a group situation, take the next step and use these tools to help your teammates through a challenging moment. If someone has a look of pain or is otherwise expressing discomfort, encourage the person to smile. It may not look very convincing at first, but, after sticking with it, he or she will soon feel the positive psychological and physiological effects. Being strong for others can help you be strong for yourself as well, and it's incredibly empowering to find that you can change your story simply by taking control of your facial and verbal expressions. You may even find the situation becoming humorous or fun for real.

BRING IT!

Bring the challenge to you. Whether you're tackling physical challenges like running a marathon or an emotional one like having a difficult conversation, you must be deliberate in your approach. I recommend pushing boundaries by structuring a minor challenge once per week—this could be something like just saying no to new obligations or adding five minutes to your usual workout routine. Then choose a monthly or quarterly challenge that requires more significant effort and planning, such as an all-day hike or attending a retreat that makes you uncomfortable (consider a silent or relationship-building retreat, each of which can be terror for many of us!). Cap it off with a good kick in the rear by choosing a gnarly challenge to tackle once a year or so.

FIND YOUR 20X FACTOR

Here are some ideas for your first 20X challenge. These may seem very difficult to accomplish—that's the point! However, you can scale them to your level of readiness. Typical disclaimers apply here—don't do anything dumb, and check with your doctor first. You can find other 20X challenge ideas at unbeatablemind.com/wostools or come up with your own.

Gnarly Physical Challenges: If you consider yourself really fit, aim high with a bid for SEALFIT Academy or Kokoro Camp, ride your bike across the country, hike the Appalachian Trail end to end, or attend the Boulder Outdoor Survival School. At home, try one thousand push-ups or pull-ups for time (don't forget to benchmark your progress as you repeat over time).

Less Gnarly Physical Challenges: Take up an endurance or extreme sport. Beginner to intermediate athletes can look to a hot yoga challenge, joining a CrossFit gym, or running a local marathon. At home, try a one-mile walking lunge.

Mighty Nonphysical Effort: Volunteer for a church mission or a traveling service unit like the Red Cross, FEMA, or Doctors Without Borders. Find a way to work with disabled veterans—I once conducted a twelve-hour challenge pairing CEOs with newly disabled warriors. Conceived as a service to the vets, it turned out to be such a powerful and life-altering experience that it was a service to the CEOs and my staff as well. Perhaps you've met someone who uprooted and went to China to teach English . . . why not you? Or sign up for a weekend doing something that makes you deeply uncomfortable. There are many opportunities out there to shatter your paradigms and lead to growth.

REFLECTIONS AND INSIGHTS _____

_____

_____

_____

_____

_____

_____

FORGE MENTAL TOUGHNESS

- The SEALs teach mental and emotional techniques to help candidates stay focused and on target during training. But it's up to the trainee to use these tools to forge their own toughness. The WOS leader will develop a daily practice to forge mental toughness using their own "big five" skills of arousal control, attention control, emotional resilience, goal setting, and visualization.

- The first premise of mental toughness is to control your response to a stimulus. That stimulus can be external, such as the shifting VUCA environment, or internal, such as fear-based chatter that distracts your focus. Training to control the breath is the WOS leader's secret weapon for controlling physiological response.

- Where you put your attention (i.e., your focus) is the second key. Once you're in control of your physiology, you can take control of your psychology with a process of feeding courage and staying focused using powerful internal dialogue.

- Emotions will torpedo even the smartest leaders, so developing emotional resilience is the next crucial skill. To do this, we harness raw emotions, transform negative

emotions that destroy performance into more positive
motivators, then build the esteem and optimism that
allow for mission success.

- Setting SMART goals chunked to the smallest arc to
success will allow you to maintain front-sight focus on
the most important targets right now, which will develop
serious momentum as the microgoals lead to an upward
success spiral.

- Visualizing your ultimate mission's victory is key to
keeping the mission clear in your broad vision while
you focus with laser-like intensity on targets in your
front sight.

RECOGNIZING STRESS SYMPTOMS

Before you can learn to control your stress response, you must learn to
recognize it. Symptoms of an overactive sympathetic nervous system
include:

- increased heart rate, respiration, and elevated blood
pressure
- upset stomach (butterflies and nausea)
- increased perspiration and sweaty palms
- dizziness
- narrowing of the auditory range and tunnel vision
- erratic sleep patterns

Think back to a time when you were stressed about something.
Did you experience these symptoms? Start paying attention to your
physical reactions whenever you're faced with a challenge or threat.
You may also notice the presence of one or more symptoms when
you're generally feeling fine—if you do, check in with yourself to see
if other symptoms are present. You may be more stressed than you
think.

TRANSFORM YOUR EMOTIONS

DIRECT works in a slightly different way when it comes to emotional control. To gain control of your feelings and transmute negative emotions into healthier expressions, you must approach the process with an attitude of acceptance—when you first detect the emotion, allow it to exist in your body. Bring your awareness to where it resides in your skin and muscles. Now, use deep breathing to get some space between you and the emotion, perhaps combined with a mantra like "I am not my thoughts and feelings." This distance will allow you to interdict and then release the emotion so you can redirect your focus and energy into a healthier expression. Communicate your new state to your subconscious through positive self-talk and simple visualization, seeing yourself in the positive emotional state you wish to achieve.

To practice doing this, see the list below of primary negative emotions and their healthier counterparts. In a quiet place, sit and relax, and then close your eyes. Try conjuring these primary negative emotions one at a time—perhaps you can recall a time when you felt anger, for example. Recall the thoughts running through your head and how you felt physically. Notice how your body, even in this exercise, begins to reproduce those same feelings. Now, DIRECT the negative emotion into a more positive expression and note how you feel physically with each shift. If it helps, conjure the memory of a time you actually felt or expressed these positive qualities to make the experience more tangible.

Primary Emotion	Healthy Expression
Anger	Clarity, determination
Fear	Alertness, eagerness
Greed	Contentment, generosity
Doubt	Curiosity, excitement
Jealousy	Acceptance, love

BOX BREATHING

Position yourself in a seated meditation or other comfortable position. Your back should be straight, your chin slightly tucked, gaze soft or eyes closed. Place your hands lightly on your knees and bring your attention to your breath.

- Slowly take a few deep diaphragm breaths, with a four-count inhalation followed immediately by a four-count complete exhalation. Repeat this for four rounds as a warm-up.

- Now, begin your Box Breathing practice by slowly taking a four-count breath through your nose.

- Hold your breath for a count of four. Concentrate on the quality of the breath and notice what enters your mind. If your mind wanders, gently bring it back to the breath.

- Slowly exhale through the nose to a count of four.

- Hold your breath again for a count of four. Pay attention to the quality of the hold and watch your mind.

Repeat this process for a minimum of five minutes, and practice it until you can do it for up to twenty minutes at a time. Over time, you can also increase the duration of the inhale, exhale, and hold periods. Seek to settle your thoughts and any fidgeting. If a thought arises, just let it go and bring your attention back to the breathing. Use Box Breathing as part of your morning ritual (see page 104) and during the day as "spot training" whenever you have the opportunity—such as when reading e-mail—or when you feel excess stress building up.

TURNING STRESS INTO SUCCESS

To control your response to stress—whether chronic, low-grade stress such as financial worries or acute, extreme stress such as with combat—you must practice and master a three-stage process. This incorporates the DIRECT process for mental control and emotional resilience (Detect, Interdict, Redirect, Energize, Communicate, and Train) from page 24 and takes it to the next level by merging it with deep breathing to control your physiological reactions.

Stage 1: As you learned to do with negative thoughts and emotions, practice the DIRECT process to perceive and interdict automatic responses to stressful events as they arise and begin expressing themselves through your mind and body.

Stage 2: Take control and reverse the sympathetic nervous system response with Box Breathing. This will prevent the retriggering of the stress response.

Stage 3: Maintain calm and focus under pressure by continuing to breathe deeply minus the box structure (no need to count or hold your breath in between inhales and exhales) while adding positive self-talk and even a quick mental projection that reinforces your self-esteem or cultivates optimism. The deep, controlled breathing process coupled with positive attention control and imagery will enable you to override any destructive thoughts or emotions sneaking in. Don't forget to monitor your responses and the language you're using to keep everything positive and healthy as per our earlier drill.

As you practice, you'll find stress dissipating in the face of improved clarity, focus, and resilience. As you recognize these developments in yourself, you'll naturally feel more confident, which continues to feed your upward spiral of success.

WHAT WOLF ARE YOU FEEDING?

Start building awareness of your mental state by forcing periodic mental breaks throughout your day. Stop whatever you're doing and quietly examine your thoughts and "feeling state" in the moment. If necessary, identify your feelings by labeling them with words such as anger, jealousy, peacefulness, excitement, and so on. If it isn't immediately obvious, you'll know whether you are stressed and feeling negative or in the flow and feeling positive once you recognize which wolf your words belong to: Courage Wolf or Fear Wolf. Once you've identified your mental and emotional state, again you will use the DIRECT process to maintain a positive mind and emotional state.

Tip 1: Place a rubber band around your wrist. Whenever you notice the rubber band, snap it and bring your attention to your thoughts and feelings at that exact moment. This is particularly useful if you're always on the go. You can substitute anything for the rubber band that will stand out to you as atypical and get your attention.

Tip 2: Set a timer (using your phone, perhaps) for every two or three hours during the day. When the timer goes off, follow the same steps as above. This is great for an office or home setting.

Tip 3: Whichever method you use, practice daily for a week, and journal your thoughts and results. When you feel yourself recognizing and DIRECTing your state of mind as it unfolds, reduce practice to three times per week, until you feel it has become a habit to recognize which wolf you're feeding moment to moment.

Day 1

_____

_____

_____

_____

_____

Day 2

_____

_____

_____

_____

Day 3

_____

_____

_____

_____

Day 4

Day 5

Day 6

Day 7

SETTING SMART GOALS

Sit quietly and contemplate your passions, values, and purpose as you defined them with Principle 1. Now consider all the things you would like to be, do, or have in your life. What about in the next year? The next five years? List them all.

- Select the three life goals or missions that most excite you and will move you toward fulfilling your purpose, then break these down further into three-year goals and one-year goals that will move you toward your primary objectives. Write these goals (read: targets) out in SMART terms: Specific, Measurable, Achievable, Relevant, and Timely or Time-Bound. Describe what it would be like to accomplish these goals and what it would be like if you do not accomplish them.

Goal 1

Specific: _____

_____

Measurable: _____

_____

Achievable: _____

_____

Relevant: _____

_____

Timely/Time-Bound: _____

_____

Goal 2

Specific: _____

Measurable: _____

Achievable: _____

Relevant: _____

Timely/Time-Bound: _____

Goal 3

Specific: _____

Measurable: _____

Achievable: _____

Relevant: _____

Timely/Time-Bound: _____

- Take a few deep breaths and get comfortable. Enter your mind gym and, using the projection screen you set up there, see yourself accomplishing these goals in as much detail as you possibly can as if you were actually living these future moments right now or as if they've already happened.

- Repeat this process for your top three quarterly or three-month microgoals, which should be tied to your selected one-year goals.

Goal 1

_____

Specific: _____

_____

Measurable: _____

_____

Achievable: _____

_____

Relevant: _____

_____

Timely/Time-Bound: _____

_____

Goal 2

_____

Specific: _____

_____

Measurable: _____

_____

Achievable: _____

_____

Relevant: _____

_____

Timely/Time-Bound: _____

_____

Goal 3

_____

Specific: _____

_____

Measurable: _____

_____

Achievable: _____

_____

Relevant: _____

_____

Timely/Time-Bound: _____

_____

When you're finished, clean up your list so you have a clear and uncluttered reference, and use the Focus Plan worksheets on pages 106–107 to organize everything and to further break down your quarterly goals into weekly and daily goals. Commit to reviewing your Focus Plans daily as part of your morning ritual.

REFLECTIONS AND INSIGHTS _____

_____

_____

_____

_____

BREAK THINGS

- For a WOS leader to excel in an accelerating world, he or she will need to learn how to break old things and remake them with new vision. Things to break include "stuck-in-a-rut" business models, processes that slow you down, services or products packaged and sold with an outdated mind-set, along with any aversion to risk that doesn't serve you any longer.

- Breaking things requires a total commitment to the new vision. To succeed at the level the Way of the SEAL requires, you can't say, "Let's see how things go"; you must burn your old boats on the shores of your new world.

- No plan survives contact with reality, and everyone has a plan until punched in the face! The WOS way is to expect, and even plan, for failure, then fail your way to success as fast as possible by systematizing trial and error and leveraging fast-twitch planning tools.

- Learning to recognize blind spots and thinking that is trapped in the past or too focused on the future will expose gaps in your competitor's plans. You will navigate these gaps for the opportunities they present, earning an advantage over those who aren't trained to move as fast as you.

- The opportunities must be capitalized on with new, visionary thinking. Innovation and rapid adaptation will allow you to test minimum viable solutions and get to a win quickly, shoring up the team's confidence and building momentum.

MAKING DECISIVENESS A HABIT

To break things with confidence, you must make decisiveness a habit. Practice with the little things. For example, the next time you're asked for your opinion, such as what movie to see or where to go for dinner, don't just pass the buck and say, "Whatever you want is fine by me." Make a decision immediately. Practice at work, too, especially when beginning a new project. Don't sit on things until you're 100 percent clear on what to do—get everyone moving with a warning order or task key players with gathering information.

MAKING VARIETY A HABIT

Make a list of all the routines in your daily and weekly life. What time do you wake? Do you brush your teeth before or after taking a shower? Do you check your e-mail before brushing your teeth? What ritual patterns of thought can you detect? We are good self-deceivers, so why don't you ask your best friend or spouse what your routine habits and thoughts are? Armed with the list, make a parallel list of ways you will break these routines. Get up at a different time every day. Take a different route to work. Do not check e-mail first thing, but only twice a day. Fast for a day or do a juice cleanse. Make a new routine out of shaking things up. This will forge new pathways in your brain, help you to avoid blind spots and rutted thinking, and spice up your life in general. You can easily apply this drill at a team level, also.

Current Routines

_____

_____

_____

_____

_____

_____

_____

_____

_____

_____

Ways to Break the Routines

_____

_____

_____

_____

_____

_____

_____

_____

_____

_____

FINDING THE SILVER LINING

This is a great tool for learning from major events and using your insights to ensure that you break things in a deliberate and powerful way rather than repeat them. It's an essential practice when you encounter a "failure," but it's also useful with a win—there's always something to learn. When your event, challenge, or mission is complete, find a quiet place. Perform deep breathing or Box Breathing to settle yourself. Now, begin by asking yourself "gratitude" questions. You've survived your attempt at or you've accomplished something big, so who can you thank and for whom are you grateful? Write them down. Certainly include yourself, but also think about your family, teammates, mentors, support staff, even your enemy. This starts you off in a positive frame of mind, which is essential for failing forward fast and breaking things effectively.

_____

_____

_____

_____

_____

_____

_____

_____

_____

_____

Next, reflect on your performance. Ask, "How did I do? What did I learn? Did I move the dial on my 20X factor? How can I improve and do even better next time? Was the event worth the time and energy—would I do it again?" Write down your reflections. You don't need to make any decisions; just make sure you write down key thoughts before they are lost or changed through the filter of memory processing.

_____

_____

_____

_____

_____

_____

_____

_____

_____

If, upon reflection, you find aspects of your performance that you are unhappy with, reframe it with a positive lesson. What did you learn? What was the silver lining? Why did it happen the way it did? Whether you won the event or not, you can guarantee that you win the aftermath with how you choose to view what happened and create a positive response to it. This very powerful process can keep you focused on feeding the Courage Wolf and the positive aspects of failure even when you fall on your face.

_____

_____

_____

_____

_____

_____

_____

_____

_____

_____

IDENTIFYING OPPORTUNITIES

This exercise will help you unlock your ability to see potential opportunities that may previously have been hidden. Answer the following questions in relationship to your field of interest:

1. Think of any prominent individuals or companies in your domain that have a past focus. Where are they stuck and what beliefs drive their behavior?

_____

_____

_____

_____

_____

2. Think of any prominent individuals or companies in your domain that have a future focus. Where are they stuck in wishful thinking, and what beliefs drive their behavior?

_____

_____

_____

_____

_____

3. Think of any prominent individuals or companies in your domain. How are they present and front-sight focused? What beliefs drive them? What can you learn from them about operating with blazing effectiveness?

_____

_____

_____

_____

_____

When you are satisfied with your answers, sit and practice your Box Breathing for a few minutes, then sit in silence for a few more. When ready, ask yourself:

1. What beliefs do I have that keep me stuck in a past focus, if any?

_____

_____

_____

_____

_____

_____

2. What beliefs do I have that keep me stuck in a future focus, if any? (Remember that you want to look toward the future but operate from the present.)

_____

_____

_____

_____

_____

_____

3. Acknowledging these beliefs and how they limit me, what opportunities open up for me in the present?

_____

_____

_____

_____

_____

4. Is it possible for me to execute on the best one of these opportunities? If not, what is holding me back? What would I need to do to move on it?

_____

_____

_____

_____

_____

Don't forget to write down any insights that come from this exercise.

_____

_____

_____

_____

_____

_____

_____

_____

_____

_____

_____

REFLECTIONS AND INSIGHTS _____

_____

_____

_____

_____

_____

_____

_____

_____

_____

_____

_____

_____

_____

_____

PRINCIPLE 7

BUILD YOUR INTUITION

- Leadership today values intuitive instinctual decisions to augment the rational, linear process. Building intuition is becoming a core skill for leading effectively in an accelerating world.

- Intuition is little understood, but the warrior has relied on it and attempted to develop it as a skill since the dawn of time. This has primarily centered around expanding the field of awareness that the leader possesses so they can recognize and understand more information and make sense of the emergent patterns.

- To develop greater awareness, the WOS leader will strengthen sensory perception through drills such as honing senses and the KIM game.

- Patterns run deep, so the WOS leader opens up to his or her inner wisdom through sense development and the silence practices. What emerges are the patterns that comprise an individual's or team's background of obviousness (BOO). This is the background programming from childhood, language, and culture that is so subtle we don't even notice it—but it's often completely obvious to those observing you closely. Clearing up BOO is one of the more challenging imperatives for the leader.

THE KIM GAME

The SEALs use a learning tool called the Keep in Memory (KIM) game to develop attention to detail and awareness and to practice accessing memory through the imprinting process. This is an excellent drill to practice Focused Awareness and Relaxed Awareness. It can be done solo but is more powerful with a team. First, choose twenty random items and place them on a floor or table under a blanket. Do not look at the items. Next, prepare yourself with a few minutes of deep breathing, clearing your mind. When you're ready, remove the blanket and study the items for sixty seconds. Shift between Relaxed Awareness and Focused Awareness to take in details and the whole. Now replace the blanket.

How many of the items can you (or your team) recall? What level of detail do you remember? Repeat this drill until you get really good at the two mental states and remember all the items with nuanced detail. Each time you practice this drill, you will improve your ability to absorb and retain information. Your field of awareness expands, and soon you will be remembering subtle and detailed information wherever you are.

_____

_____

_____

_____

_____

_____

_____

_____

_____

_____

HONE YOUR SENSES

Take a moment to cup your ears and close your eyes. Now just listen and notice what comes up. Your breathing will probably sound like a freight train at first, and you may see images and flashing lights. A moment before, you weren't even aware of these internal things! Think of this training as your personal sensory-deprivation tank. (And if you have access to one of those, by all means use it. In fact, any endeavor that plunges you into deep silence—such as scuba diving, rock climbing, parachuting, or cross-country skiing—will heighten this sensory perception.) In the darkness, without noise or visual references, you can get into a deep state of sensory awareness and mindfulness where everything that goes on internally is a big deal. Next, remove your hands from your ears. Just sit quietly and listen. Jot down what you initially hear . . . then listen more intently. What else do you hear now? Then do it again and yet again. You will note layers upon layers of noises that your brain previously shunted to your subconscious because they were deemed irrelevant.

You can repeat this drill for each of your five senses by following a pattern of deprivation and then intently focusing and going deeper into the isolated sense. For example, what do you see when you shut your eyes or are in total darkness? When you open them, what do you see first? When you look more closely, what do you notice?

_____

_____

_____

_____

_____

_____

_____

_____

_____

_____

AWAKEN YOUR INTUITION

Using the process described on page 25, enter your mind gym and just be present there for a few moments. Express gratitude for having this place to train mentally and for all you have in your life. Next, invite your counselor into the mind gym. You don't have to know who this is in advance; in fact, it's better if you don't have a rational concept of who this is—just see who shows up! When I did this, an older man with the strength of a warrior—who I believe was an Apache scout—appeared. He continues to be my counselor to this day. When your counselor arrives, thank him or her, invite him or her to sit with you, and then ask your question. Don't expect to start having a conversation right away, though many of my students admit to rewarding exchanges with their counselors, who impart knowledge that was previously unknown to them. Instead, you may receive images, a flood of emotion, or just a strong sense of the right answer. When you're finished, be sure you thank your counselor for his or her time.

In a tight spot, if you've analyzed a situation and are unsure of the way forward, try carefully constructing a simple yes or no question that will answer the issue. State it positively, and affirm that you are asking your inner self for the good of all concerned. Feel a burning desire to know the best answer to this question; don't waste energy ammo on frivolous questions or on issues you don't really care about. Then take your question into your mind gym.

Some advanced tips to help ensure the effectiveness of your mind gym practice:

1. Before you enter your mind gym to visualize a goal, be very clear on what you desire and articulate it in positive terms as if it has already happened. Then infuse the visualization with the belief that the process is helping you achieve that goal.

2. Be consistent between what you seek to achieve in your visualization and what your BOO beliefs are telling you. If you visualize a financial goal, but in your subconscious mind you tell yourself you can't afford it or don't deserve it, then you will cancel the positive benefits of the visualization. You must eliminate any beliefs that contradict your desired outcomes before embarking on

the visualization. In this case, you will want to use the
mind gym to uncover your BOO and also to plant seeds
of worthiness before returning to the work of seeing,
believing, and making it happen.

3. You must develop the subtle ability to recognize and receive
   information from the subconscious. This is hard at first but
   will come with practice and with experience if you approach
   the mind gym technique with openness. The process of
   inviting a "counselor" into your mind gym can help.

4. You will want to take action on synchronicities that occur
   and doors that open to you after completing a mind gym
   practice. Once you open to your inner wisdom and learn
   to control the imprinting of your subconscious mind
   through positive visualization, insights will flow forth
   more easily, and the universe often seems to conspire
   with your subconscious for the win!

CLEARING OUT YOUR BOO

Use the same process as on page 25 to quiet yourself and enter your mind gym. Once there, state your intention to explore your
BOO. Now, instead of projecting onto your mental screen an image
of your desired future, allow your mind to scan back in time to events
in your life that were uncomfortable, distasteful, or flat-out painful.
If there's a specific incident you want to revisit, you can go straight
there. Otherwise, just allow whatever comes up to become your point
of focus. (Alternatively, you can begin with a particular behavior or
event in mind.) When your mind settles on a time and place, let the
images on the screen slow to a crawl and then merge with the imagery
as if you had traveled back in time. Embody the experience with all
your senses as though you were living through it again right now.

Note any sensations and emotions that arise in your body, especially noting where they show up and what level or degree of discomfort they cause. These responses are clues that will help you identify
where negative emotional energy is stored and how intense it is. The

location becomes the point of focus for your awareness during the remainder of the exercise. For instance, you may experience a sick feeling in the pit of your stomach, or you may notice your heart racing as your chest tightens. The intensity will indicate the severity of the issue. Rate how intense your response is on a scale of 1 to 10, 1 being not very intense and 10 very intense. If a response elicits a rating of 10, this issue affects you very deeply, and you will need to spend a lot of time working on it. If it elicits a rating of 2, you can deal with it more quickly then move on.

Next, bring the younger version of you into the present to meet the current you in your mind gym. In other words, if the painful event happened when you were ten years old, visualize your ten-year-old self standing before you. When you can clearly see your younger self, talk to him or her about the inciting event. Say that everything is okay now—it wasn't their fault, it's over, and all is forgiven. Tell him or her that it's okay to release the pain and let the upset feelings go. You may even want to imagine hugging your younger self or offering comfort in some other way. Finally, before you gratefully say goodbye to your younger self, ask him or her to integrate with your current self. You may receive agreement or you could even go so far as to visualize your two bodies merging into one.

If this all sounds silly to you, just do the best you can. Trust me, it is a powerful exercise. When I did this for a painful incident in my own life, my younger self felt so relieved, he jumped up and down and started doing cartwheels!

The final step in this exercise is to bring the original event back up on the screen in your mind gym and again visualize your younger self and any other involved parties. Let the scene play out, noticing any differences in imagery or how you feel. Does your younger self appear less stressed? Is his or her body language more powerful and confident? Do the other parties to the event look less intimidating or angry? Bring your awareness to the location in which you identified stored emotion—how does it feel now? Rate the intensity again and compare to your initial rating. You should feel a decrease, even if only a little. You will want to repeat this process for this specific event until your younger self appears whole and healthy, the third parties no longer pose a threat, and your stored negative emotions have dissipated (meaning the intensity now ranks a 1 or 0).

It's very possible that some BOO issues will be too deeply rooted or scary for you to get at yourself, so you may need a trained therapist to assist you. I recommend you seek someone trained in EMDR (emdr.com), a therapeutic process that approaches BOO work through the nervous system. FOR YOUR SAFETY: If you were severely physically or emotionally abused in childhood, do not try to "self-medicate" using this drill without the support of a professional.

AUTHENTIC COMMUNICATION

This practice is very powerful for building your intuition muscles as you expand your awareness with regard to both how other people express their feelings nonverbally and how you do the same. The essence is to maintain a Focused Awareness on what your communication partner is saying while maintaining a Relaxed Awareness on your thoughts and feelings in response to what he or she is communicating. Note that you will get better at this internal awareness as a natural outgrowth of deepening your sensory awareness and emotional resilience. Then, when you feel the need to speak (which, incidentally will be much less often when you do this practice routinely), you will pause before you respond then open your mouth to speak only if:

- what you have to say is truthful
- what you have to say adds value and is helpful to the conversation
- what you have to say is positive and comes from a place of respect and genuine concern for the other party

REFLECTIONS AND INSIGHTS _____

_____

_____

_____

THINK OFFENSE, ALL THE TIME

- Leading in an accelerating world can't be a defensive act. The WOS leader must learn to think offensively as the new normal. For this to happen, an unwavering confidence in one's own vision and the power of the team to mobilize toward that vision are key.

- Unwavering confidence starts with thoughts and emotions but is projected through words and actions. Changing our words to be more offense-oriented will telegraph more powerful action both internally and externally.

- Threats are all around us, but it is the prepared leader who sees them first and avoids them rather than having to fight a way through. Cultivating a radar-like mindset that constantly scans for threats is the SEAL way. This skill will serve you well when travelling to unstable countries and will help you protect your company, team, and family from predators.

- SEALs never do the expected and neither should you. Break your patterns of thinking and acting to keep things fresh, always learning and growing, and keep those watching you (like your competitors) off balance.

- An "offense, all the time" mind-set is agile and able to accelerate into a challenge. This velocity speeds up the OODA loop decision process and keeps you ahead of the competition in a state of dynamic stability where you are changing as fast as the changes around you.

CHANGE YOUR WORDS, CHANGE YOUR ATTITUDE

Make an honest assessment of the language that you use on a daily basis. Do you use negative or "slow down" words? Note the imagery that the words in the first column of the list below conjure up in your mind. Now compare these with the images conjured up by the words in the second column. Major difference, right? Write down any other defensive or negative words you use on a regular basis, and write a positive word or phrase to replace it. Repeat the imagery exercise with your own two columns to make sure you're on the right track. Practice using the new language daily, and journal your findings every week. Keep at this until it becomes a new habit and second nature.

Defend	Attack
Good	Great
Block	Strike
Retreat	Pounce
Can't	Will
Try	Do
Failed	Learned
Maybe	Definitely
_____	_____
_____	_____
_____	_____
_____	_____
_____	_____

KNOWING WHEN TO BREAK THE RULES

Use the questions below to define some boundaries for which rules to break and when to break them:

1. Is the rule ethical in your definition of what is ethical?

_____

_____

_____

_____

_____

2. Is the rule legal in your legal system?

_____

_____

_____

_____

_____

3. What is the upside you will potentially see by breaking the rule?

_____

_____

_____

_____

_____

4. Will breaking the rule land you in serious trouble if caught by "the authorities"?

_____

_____

_____

_____

_____

5. Is it better to beg forgiveness than to ask permission in this case?

_____

_____

_____

_____

_____

6. Will anyone get hurt if you break the rule?

_____

_____

_____

_____

_____

7. If someone could get hurt, is it only the bad guys?

_____

_____

_____

_____

_____

8. What's the worst thing that could happen—what would the consequences be if you read about it in the _New York Times_ the next day?

_____

_____

_____

_____

_____

YELLOW RADAR

Use this exercise to practice maintaining a "yellow state" of passive alertness. For example, when going to a restaurant, ensure that your yellow radar is switched "on." Scan the environment outside the restaurant and see what you notice. Try to note how many people are there, what they are wearing, and look for patterns. Then scan for anything that does not fit the pattern. For example, is there anyone waiting to eat alone? Is there someone standing around who doesn't look like he or she is engaged in going somewhere or doing something? Without being paranoid, just notice if there is anything unusual and use your gut to feel the surroundings.

When you enter the restaurant, scan the inside just as you did the outside. Note patterns and anything that doesn't fit. Ask the host for a seat near the back of the restaurant, where you can casually observe while you are enjoying your meal. Keep a mental log of the activities during the time at the restaurant. Maintain your passive-alert "yellow" state of awareness throughout your time there. Repeat this drill when you go to the movies, shopping, to the bank, and so on, and eventually it will become a permanent state of elevated awareness that will serve you well at home, at work, when traveling, and even when out on the town.

DEVELOP YOUR STANDARD OPERATING PROCEDURES

When thinking offensively, you're preparing for the future and focusing on your ability to act quickly and smoothly in the moment. To identify what aspects of your business you can turn into standard operating procedures, ask the following questions:

- What processes or activities do I or my team perform repeatedly?

_____

_____

_____

_____

_____

• What are the critical nodes of those processes?

_____

_____

_____

_____

_____

• What core tasks related to these critical nodes are
  repeatable, measurable, and trainable?

_____

_____

_____

_____

_____

Now write your SOPs down step by step and develop a simple training plan around them for your operators. For maximum success, use the crawl, walk, run model: Seek accuracy in the task one time initially, followed by accuracy at a moderate pace, and then finally aim for accurate execution with velocity. Don't forget to build in redundancy in case of unexpected problems—remember, the world is unpredictable, but destiny favors the prepared.

_____

_____

_____

_____

_____

_____

_____

_____

_____

_____

_____

_____

_____

_____

_____

_____

_____

_____

_____

_____

OODA LOOP

The OODA loop is a rapid planning tool—recall its original intention for air-to-air combat. For business leaders, the tool is best used when you are pressured to make quick decisions in a fluid environment.

Observe your position relative to the competition. How is their next move going to affect you? Use your situational awareness skills to look at the details as well as the big picture. For example, your product is first to market and superior in quality yet on the pricey side of the market range. You observe your competition introduce a lower-priced knockoff, and you expect them to overtake you.

Orient to the new reality you've observed as fast as possible without making a move (yet). What is your goal—for example, to beat out the competition and regain market share at any cost or to maintain quality, which may mean exploring new markets that appreciate value and are less price sensitive, abandoning the product line to explore a new one, or finding new ways to educate your customers about the value? What effect will lowering your price have on your margins? How will your competition respond—will they start a price war, and what will that mean for your company? Orientation is processing and analyzing the gathered intelligence quickly relative to your normal planning cycle. In a SEAL op, the OODA loop is almost real time. For a company, it may mean collapsing your planning cycles from months to days or weeks.

Decide on an action. This is where the rubber meets the road. Acting on a good decision is better than not acting on a great decision. So make a good decision, one that speeds up your OODA loop, while offering the potential to slow down the other players in your cat-and-mouse game. In our example, you decide to back your product with an information campaign emphasizing the superior quality and prestige of ownership to differentiate it in the market. Simultaneously, you file for intellectual property protection and enlist the support of your loyal customers to blog about how amazing your product is and to be wary of the knockoffs.

Act and instantly seek feedback. Monitor the thought-leader blogs in your space, and watch for any reaction from your competition. Learn from any feedback, reset your observation post, and continue cycling through the loop.

REFLECTIONS AND INSIGHTS _____

_____

_____

_____

_____

_____

_____

_____

_____

_____

_____

_____

_____

_____

_____

_____

_____

_____

_____

_____

_____

_____

_____

_____

_____

_____

_____

_____

_____

_____

_____

_____

_____

_____

_____

_____

_____

_____

_____

TRAINING IN THE WAY OF THE SEAL

- The principles outlined in this book are meant for reflection and action, but the exercise and drills are meant for daily training and practice. You will not be able to master them in a moment—rather, employ a "slow is smooth, smooth is fast" approach to integrating them into your daily, weekly, monthly, and quarterly routines.

- The WOS integrated vertical development training is summarized with examples from Mark and his team. Use these as a template for creating your own training plan that fits with your needs, interest, and time constraints. A great WOS training plan would be a full hour between the morning and evening rituals and spot drills.

- It's better to train for twenty minutes a day (forever) than put in a ton of time up front and leave all this behind when some obstacle or, more likely, some new shiny book comes out. The concepts and tools in this book have stood the test of time, work if you work them, and are not quick hacks to improve your performance. The goal is total transformation to tap your 20X potential and to serve the world boldly as a world-centric, elite warrior-leader.

Your Way of the SEAL Training Plan

Now that you have a clear picture of what you're already doing and what you need, check out the Training Tools at a Glance on the following pages. You'll note that every drill, exercise, or practice listed is marked to show its role in developing each mountain and WOS principle. I also suggest how much time to devote to each. Browse the list, and use your self-assessment to guide you in selecting the right tools and practices for you in the development of your WOS training plan. In general, if the suggested frequency offers a range, choose the amount of training time based on your experience with that activity and with your needs. For example, if you're an experienced visualizer, you may only choose to incorporate a brief "Future Me" visualization into your day, whereas someone new to the concept of envisioning should probably devote fifteen minutes or more daily to strengthen that muscle and their mental toughness.

The bulk of your training plan will be daily tasks planned in a weekly format. There are a few additional weekly, monthly, quarterly, and annual components. The daily tasks in my plan take me two to three hours to complete (most of that is my physical training, which is key for my lifestyle and career and accordingly commands the lion's share of my daily training time). If you have less time to devote to your training, your plan must adjust accordingly—with slightly less focus on physical training, you could still accomplish everything in an hour or two. Fill in the components of your weekly training plan on the chart on pages 88–89. Refresh you plan with every quarterly and annual review. You'll find extra charts to fill in on pages 236–241 if needed.

Notes on Training Tools at a Glance:

1. Foundational elements are marked with an asterisk. These are key components for all WOS leaders, regardless of where you are with your training, though your experience and needs may dictate how often you incorporate them.

2. Time requirements indicate a suggested range along which you will choose a time commitment that is appropriate to your schedule and development needs. If no time frame is

Training Tools at a Glance

Drill/Exercise/ Ritual	WOS Principle/Skill	Time Requirement	Physical
WOS Assessment*	Establish Your Set Point	Check in monthly for needed updates/changes	
"Envision Your Future Me"*	Establish Your Set Point	5–15 minutes daily	
Still Water Runs Deep*	Develop Front-Sight Focus	5–15 minutes daily	
Fantasizing with Purpose (aka "practice visualization")	Develop Front-Sight Focus	5–15 minutes daily	
The Sentinel at the Gate*	Develop Front-Sight Focus	1 minute several times a day	
DIRECT Your Mind*	Develop Front-Sight Focus	1 minute several times a day	
KISS*	Develop Front-Sight Focus	5–15 minutes monthly	
The Idea Lab	Bulletproof Your Mission	5–15 minutes as needed	
Transmuting Pain into Positivity	Do Today What Others Won't	5 minutes as needed	X

listed, it means there is no minimum requirement. Feel free to increase the time you spend on an activity as you need or want to. You may also find that some activities, such as the KISS or DIRECT processes, may need more frequent practice early in your training but can be performed with less frequency once the concepts they embody become habit.

3. This matrix does not include tools (such as the mission planning tools of Principle 3) because these aren't trained or practiced per se.

Mental	Emotional	Intuition	Spirit	Page
X	X		X	7
X		X	X	16
X	X	X	X	20
X				20
X	X	X		23
X	X	X		24
X	X		X	26
X		X		34
X	X			40

Training Tools at a Glance (*continued*)

Drill/Exercise/ Ritual	WOS Principle/Skill	Time Requirement	Physical
Bring It!	Do Today What Others Won't	Weekly or monthly	X
Find Your 20X Factor*	Do Today What Others Won't	Quarterly or annually	X
Transform Your Emotions*	Forge Mental Toughness	As needed	
Box Breathing*	Forge Mental Toughness	5–15 minutes daily	X
Turning Stress into Success*	Forge Mental Toughness	5–15 minutes as needed	X
What Wolf Are You Feeding?*	Forge Mental Toughness	1 minute several times a day	X
Setting SMART Goals*	Forge Mental Toughness	Check in daily and review / update monthly, quarterly, and annually	
Making Decisiveness a Habit	Break Things	As needed	
Making Variety a Habit	Break Things	As needed	
Finding the Silver Lining*	Break Things	1–2 minutes daily or as needed	
Identifying Opportunities	Break Things	10–20 minutes quarterly	
The KIM Game	Build Your Intuition	5–15 minutes weekly	
Hone Your Senses	Build Your Intuition	5–15 minutes weekly	
Awaken Your Intuition*	Build Your Intuition	5–15 minutes as needed	
Authentic Communication*	Build Your Intuition	10–30 minutes daily	
Change Your Words, Change Your Attitude*	Think Offense	As needed	
Yellow Radar*	Think Offense, All the Time	Periodically	
SEALFIT, CrossFit, or similar*	functional fitness	60 minutes/ 3–5 times a week	X
Sacred Silence (Still Water Runs Deep or other meditation)*	mindfulness/awareness	5–15 minutes as needed	
Somatic Practice (yoga, qi gong, tai chi, dance)*	mindfulness/awareness	5–15 minutes daily and up to 60 minutes 2–3 times a week	X
Positive Self-Talk & Mantra*	positive self-talk/attention control	As needed	
Focus Planning & Goal Review*		5–15 minutes daily	
Professional Therapy*		60 minutes as needed (minimum annually)	

Mental	Emotional	Intuition	Spirit	Page
X	X			40
X	X		X	40
	X			45
X		X	X	45
X				46
X	X			47
X				50
X	X			56
X	X			56
X	X			57
X				59
X				64
		X		65
		X		66
X	X	X	X	70
X	X	X		73
X	X	X		76
X				
X	X	X	X	
X	X	X	X	
X	X		X	
X				
X	X	X	X	

Weekly Training Plan

Time	Monday	Tuesday	Wednesday

Thursday	Friday	Saturday	Sunday

REFLECTIONS AND INSIGHTS _____

_____

_____

_____

_____

_____

_____

_____

_____

_____

_____

_____

_____

_____

_____

_____

_____

_____

_____

_____

_____

_____

_____

_____

_____

_____

_____

_____

_____

THE SECRETS OF ELITE TEAMS

- Your journey as a WOS leader will not be a solo one. You need to build an elite team inspired by your vision, aligned with your culture, and capable of executing the mission. This is not easy to do, but there are some simple rules to follow.

- An elite team has spirit and not just a "we won the game" kind of spirit. It's a palpable energy field created when everyone is in flow. This team flow will magnify power exponentially.

- The team must start developing this team flow by knowing its purpose, its why, and forging a team ethos. Sharing values and vision is crucial for an elite team's members to connect their personal lives to the team life.

- The mind-set that ensues is a "together we grow" mind-set where each teammate is challenging and supporting the others to vertically develop new capacities and horizontally build new skills. This creates an environment of constant momentum and a relentless focus on training skills and character. Everyone becomes an "owner" and cares for the mission, team, and structure.

- Hiring to achieve a team like this must be an attractive force rather than a sales pitch. The individuals who become Navy SEALs do so in part because they know, beyond a shadow of doubt, that the organization is right for them because they already share the SEAL ethos.

• When a team attracts for character and trains for skill, trust goes up dramatically. Trust is the glue that holds a team together, so elite teams take it very seriously by training it, demanding it, and removing teammates who violate it. This requires a communication strategy of brutal honesty and debriefing every mess-up with an attitude of improving the entire team's mission focus. The team works together as a "team of teams" with a structure that has a high degree of integrity, but almost unlimited flexibility.

INTEGRATED PERSPECTIVE TAKING AND MAKING

Imagine that your office has become extremely dependent on its sole contracting expert. If she left, it would be nearly impossible to replace her, and your organization would be in serious trouble. You were in a meeting with senior management where they discussed their belief that she isn't promotable, and they made it very clear this information was not to leave the room. Then one day, this contracting expert comes to you for career advice. Take the following perspectives and write two to three sentences describing each person's view of the situation.

• the contracting expert

_____

_____

_____

_____

_____

• a supervisor/team leader

_____

_____

_____

_____

_____

• an employee/staff member

_____

_____

_____

_____

_____

_____

• senior management

_____

_____

_____

_____

_____

• the organization

_____

_____

_____

_____

_____

• other

_____

_____

_____

_____

_____

Discuss these perspectives with your teammates, then break into two teams. Each team should use 10 minutes to come up with a solution that takes into account as many of the perspectives as possible.

• **Step 1:** Discuss how to and then coordinate all the
perspectives into a response to the dilemma. What
framework, method, or criteria do you want to use?

_____

_____

_____

_____

_____

• **Step 2:** Coordinate the perspectives following your plan
from Step 1.

_____

_____

_____

_____

_____

• **Step 3:** Have each group present its solution in a few
sentences.

_____

_____

_____

_____

_____

• What action would you take and why?

_____

_____

_____

_____

_____

• How does this approach take into account as many perspectives as possible?

_____

_____

_____

_____

_____

• What principles guided your approach?

_____

_____

_____

_____

_____

DEVELOPING A TEAM ETHOS

You've done a lot of work on your personal ethos, which will have a powerful impact on how you see your role as a leader. Everyone on an elite team will have some form of personal ethos, even if they haven't articulated it yet as you have. But as we've learned, the collective is greater than the sum of its parts, and a team with clarity around its purpose (vision), targets (mission), and principles (values or stand) will outperform all others. This is a team reflection and alignment exercise that requires some preparation and then a couple hours to do well.

Step 1: Ask your teammates to read Principle 1 and this chapter, then think about the team's purpose, targets, and values. Where do they stand from their unique perspective? Set a meeting to synchronize and align these perspectives into a single statement of your team ethos, your overarching "why" that will guide alignment of intent with action.

Step 2: Start the meeting with Box Breathing, then visualize together your team accomplishing its mission powerfully, with every teammate fully engaged, employing kokoro (the merging of your heart and mind in action) in decisions, and acting with three-sphere alignment.

Step 3: Have each member present his or her thoughts on the three elements of ethos from step 1. That includes you! No action is necessary at this stage—just authentic listening.

Step 4: Facilitate in pulling together the common themes from each teammate's presentations and, with input, draft a single statement.

_____

_____

_____

_____

_____

_____

_____

_____

_____

_____

_____

_____

_____

_____

_____

_____

_____

_____

_____

Step 5: Adjourn the meeting. Send out the results for review and discussion among your teammates. Remember, this is a living team ethos, not meant to be dictated by you or fixed forever. It is meant to evolve.

WHAT'S YOUR MISSION?

Is your mission framed in simple terms with the right targets selected in the right order for the right reasons? Redo the above exercise, but this time have your teammates read Principles 2 and 3 and use the FITS, PROP, and SMACC tools to refine your team's or organization's mission focus.

_____

_____

_____

_____

_____

_____

_____

_____

_____

_____

_____

_____

_____

_____

_____

_____

_____

_____

_____

_____

CREATING YOUR SELECTION PROCESS

Do you recruit or attract employees? Do you hire for talent or character? Employees—your team—are the most important component of your business. Get the right teammates aligned with the vision and mission, and the customers, shareholders, community, and world will all be taken care of.

Take a moment to reflect on your hiring process. Do you use attractive statements, stories, and images that project your ethos or "why" rather than some industrial age "what we do"? How do you select for character and ensure a path into or out of the culture depending upon fit?

_____

_____

_____

_____

_____

_____

_____

_____

_____

_____

STRUCTURAL INTEGRITY

Look into your processes, space, and rules. What is holding up a team of teams from spontaneously arising to dominate a challenge or mission? How is trust generated and developed, and how are teammates held accountable? How is ownership of the mission thwarted or rewarded? Where, when, and how does the team train together to develop vertically and deepen respect and trust? Are they rewarded for training personally and serving outside the organization? Are you following the principles of B corporations or "conscious capitalism"? What rules exist about communication that may hold back authenticity and trust?

_____

_____

_____

_____

_____

_____

_____

_____

_____

_____

REFLECTIONS AND INSIGHTS _____

_____

_____

_____

_____

_____

_____

_____

_____

_____

_____

_____

_____

_____

_____

_____

_____

_____

_____

_____

_____

_____

_____

_____

_____

FOCUS PLANS AND POWER RITUALS

Checking in with your focus plans regularly will lead you to take powerful KISS actions every day. You won't waste time on anything that doesn't move you toward your goals. When you get superfocused every day, week, month/quarter, and year on those top two or three things that are connected to your passion, purpose, and mission, your thoughts and actions naturally align. When you're in alignment, it's easier to stack up victories, which develops confidence, which in turn supports your simplifying efforts, and so on in an upward cycle of success!

Similarly, performing Power Rituals daily and as needed before and after major events (be it a big race or a presentation at work) helps train your mind to start and end each day and each important challenge in a positive, powerful "performance zone" state.

In this section, I've given you two weeks' worth of worksheets for your Morning Ritual, Daily/Weekly Focus Plan, and Evening Ritual, along with three copies of Pre-Event and Post-Event Ritual worksheets and three years' worth of Quarterly and Annual Focus Plans. You'll also find additional Weekly Training Plan charts here if you need to tweak your plan.

If you need additional copies of any worksheet, feel free to photocopy them as many times as you need. With each one, don't forget to fill in the appropriate date, month, quarter, or year.

Morning Ritual for_____

When you awake in the morning, the first thing you will do is drink a large glass of fresh water, and then sit comfortably with your journal in a quiet space—preferably one dedicated to your reflective and visualization work—and ask yourself the following empowering questions. Write down whatever comes up.

- What and whom am I grateful for today?

_____

_____

_____

_____

_____

_____

- What am I excited about and looking forward to doing today?

_____

_____

_____

_____

_____

_____

- What is my purpose, and do my plans for today connect me to it?

_____

_____

_____

_____

• How can I move the dial toward my goals today?

_____

_____

_____

_____

_____

_____

• To whom can I reach out and serve or thank today?

_____

_____

_____

_____

_____

_____

• Are my goals still aligned with my purpose?

_____

_____

_____

_____

_____

_____

_____

Next, spend a minimum of five minutes Box Breathing, then spend a minimum of five minutes in mindful movement (I do up to an hour some days). My preference is yoga, but tai chi, qi gong, or a short mindful walk will work. Finally, before you start your day, review your Daily or Weekly Focus Plan. Make any adjustments to ensure it's in alignment with the answers to your morning questions, and block time in your schedule for key project work or training.

Daily/Weekly Focus Plan for _____

The One Thing (the most important thing I will achieve this day and/
or week):

_____

_____

_____

_____

_____

Priority Tasks (that I must complete today or this week): _____

_____

_____

_____

_____

_____

Projects (to work on one step at a minimum each day): _____

_____

_____

_____

_____

_____

Contacts (calls/e-mails to people I need to connect with): _____

_____

_____

_____

_____

_____

_____

Habit (what am I working on this week, and how): _____

_____

_____

_____

_____

_____

_____

Notes, Ideas, and Inspirations (any ideas that came up during the morning ritual): _____

_____

_____

_____

_____

_____

_____

_____

_____

_____

_____

_____

_____

_____

_____

_____

_____

_____

_____

_____

Evening Ritual for _____

Before you settle in for the night, sit comfortably with your journal in a quiet space—preferably one dedicated to your reflective and visualization work—and ask yourself the following empowering questions. Write down whatever comes up.

_____

_____

_____

_____

_____

_____

- Was I "on" and in the zone today or "off" and unbalanced?

_____

_____

_____

_____

_____

_____

_____

- What contributed to this feeling?

_____

_____

_____

_____

_____

_____

_____

_____

- What were the top three positive things I accomplished or that happened today? What did I learn from them?

_____

_____

_____

_____

_____

- Are there unsolved challenges I would like my subconscious mind to help me solve tonight?

_____

_____

_____

_____

_____

_____

_____

- What went wrong today and what is the silver lining?

_____

_____

_____

_____

_____

_____

Now enter a meditative state using Box Breathing, and then enter your mind gym in order to review your major goals and continue your ongoing visualization work. While in your mind gym, put any questions or problems that are bugging you to your counselor or to your subconscious. Pay attention to your dreams and any waking thoughts the next day—the answer will usually be there for you.

Morning Ritual for_____

When you awake in the morning, the first thing you will do is drink a large glass of fresh water, and then sit comfortably with your journal in a quiet space—preferably one dedicated to your reflective and visualization work—and ask yourself the following empowering questions. Write down whatever comes up.

- What and whom am I grateful for today?

_____

_____

_____

_____

_____

_____

_____

- What am I excited about and looking forward to doing today?

_____

_____

_____

_____

_____

_____

- What is my purpose, and do my plans for today connect me to it?

_____

_____

_____

- How can I move the dial toward my goals today?

_____

_____

_____

_____

_____

_____

- To whom can I reach out and serve or thank today?

_____

_____

_____

_____

_____

_____

- Are my goals still aligned with my purpose?

_____

_____

_____

_____

_____

_____

Next, spend a minimum of five minutes Box Breathing, then spend a minimum of five minutes in mindful movement (I do up to an hour some days). My preference is yoga, but tai chi, qi gong, or a short mindful walk will work. Finally, before you start your day, review your Daily or Weekly Focus Plan. Make any adjustments to ensure it's in alignment with the answers to your morning questions, and block time in your schedule for key project work or training.

Daily/Weekly Focus Plan for _____

The One Thing (the most important thing I will achieve this day and/
or week):

_____

_____

_____

_____

_____

Priority Tasks (that I must complete today or this week): _____

_____

_____

_____

_____

_____

Projects (to work on one step at a minimum each day): _____

_____

_____

_____

_____

_____

Contacts (calls/e-mails to people I need to connect with): _____

_____

_____

_____

_____

_____

_____

Habit (what am I working on this week, and how): _____

_____

_____

_____

_____

_____

_____

Notes, Ideas, and Inspirations (any ideas that came up during the morning ritual): _____

Evening Ritual for _____

Before you settle in for the night, sit comfortably with your journal in a quiet space—preferably one dedicated to your reflective and visualization work—and ask yourself the following empowering questions. Write down whatever comes up.

_____

_____

_____

_____

_____

_____

- Was I "on" and in the zone today or "off" and unbalanced?

_____

_____

_____

_____

_____

_____

_____

- What contributed to this feeling?

_____

_____

_____

_____

_____

_____

_____

- What were the top three positive things I accomplished or that happened today? What did I learn from them?

_____

_____

_____

_____

_____

- Are there unsolved challenges I would like my subconscious mind to help me solve tonight?

_____

_____

_____

_____

_____

_____

_____

- What went wrong today and what is the silver lining?

_____

_____

_____

_____

_____

Now enter a meditative state using Box Breathing, and then enter your mind gym in order to review your major goals and continue your ongoing visualization work. While in your mind gym, put any questions or problems that are bugging you to your counselor or to your subconscious. Pay attention to your dreams and any waking thoughts the next day—the answer will usually be there for you.

Morning Ritual for_____

When you awake in the morning, the first thing you will do is drink a large glass of fresh water, and then sit comfortably with your journal in a quiet space—preferably one dedicated to your reflective and visualization work—and ask yourself the following empowering questions. Write down whatever comes up.

• What and whom am I grateful for today?

_____

_____

_____

_____

_____

_____

_____

• What am I excited about and looking forward to doing today?

_____

_____

_____

_____

_____

_____

• What is my purpose, and do my plans for today connect me to it?

_____

_____

_____

_____

• How can I move the dial toward my goals today?

_____

_____

_____

_____

_____

_____

• To whom can I reach out and serve or thank today?

_____

_____

_____

_____

_____

_____

• Are my goals still aligned with my purpose?

_____

_____

_____

_____

_____

_____

Next, spend a minimum of five minutes Box Breathing, then spend a minimum of five minutes in mindful movement (I do up to an hour some days). My preference is yoga, but tai chi, qi gong, or a short mindful walk will work. Finally, before you start your day, review your Daily or Weekly Focus Plan. Make any adjustments to ensure it's in alignment with the answers to your morning questions, and block time in your schedule for key project work or training.

Daily/Weekly Focus Plan for _____

The One Thing (the most important thing I will achieve this day and/or week):

_____

_____

_____

_____

_____

Priority Tasks (that I must complete today or this week): _____

_____

_____

_____

_____

_____

Projects (to work on one step at a minimum each day): _____

_____

_____

_____

_____

_____

Contacts (calls/e-mails to people I need to connect with): _____

_____

_____

_____

_____

_____

_____

Habit (what am I working on this week, and how): _____

_____

_____

_____

_____

_____

_____

Notes, Ideas, and Inspirations (any ideas that came up during the morning ritual): _____

_____

_____

_____

_____

_____

_____

_____

_____

_____

_____

_____

_____

_____

_____

_____

_____

_____

_____

Evening Ritual for _____

Before you settle in for the night, sit comfortably with your journal in a quiet space—preferably one dedicated to your reflective and visualization work—and ask yourself the following empowering questions. Write down whatever comes up.

_____

_____

_____

_____

_____

_____

- Was I "on" and in the zone today or "off" and unbalanced?

_____

_____

_____

_____

_____

_____

_____

- What contributed to this feeling?

_____

_____

_____

_____

_____

_____

_____

_____

- What were the top three positive things I accomplished or that happened today? What did I learn from them?

_____

_____

_____

_____

_____

- Are there unsolved challenges I would like my subconscious mind to help me solve tonight?

_____

_____

_____

_____

_____

_____

_____

- What went wrong today and what is the silver lining?

_____

_____

_____

_____

_____

Now enter a meditative state using Box Breathing, and then enter your mind gym in order to review your major goals and continue your ongoing visualization work. While in your mind gym, put any questions or problems that are bugging you to your counselor or to your subconscious. Pay attention to your dreams and any waking thoughts the next day—the answer will usually be there for you.

Morning Ritual for_____

When you awake in the morning, the first thing you will do is drink a large glass of fresh water, and then sit comfortably with your journal in a quiet space—preferably one dedicated to your reflective and visualization work—and ask yourself the following empowering questions. Write down whatever comes up.

- What and whom am I grateful for today?

_____

_____

_____

_____

_____

_____

_____

- What am I excited about and looking forward to doing today?

_____

_____

_____

_____

_____

_____

- What is my purpose, and do my plans for today connect me to it?

_____

_____

_____

_____

• How can I move the dial toward my goals today?

_____

_____

_____

_____

_____

_____

• To whom can I reach out and serve or thank today?

_____

_____

_____

_____

_____

_____

• Are my goals still aligned with my purpose?

_____

_____

_____

_____

_____

_____

Next, spend a minimum of five minutes Box Breathing, then spend a minimum of five minutes in mindful movement (I do up to an hour some days). My preference is yoga, but tai chi, qi gong, or a short mindful walk will work. Finally, before you start your day, review your Daily or Weekly Focus Plan. Make any adjustments to ensure it's in alignment with the answers to your morning questions, and block time in your schedule for key project work or training.

Daily/Weekly Focus Plan for _____

The One Thing (the most important thing I will achieve this day and/or week):

_____

_____

_____

_____

_____

Priority Tasks (that I must complete today or this week): _____

_____

_____

_____

_____

_____

Projects (to work on one step at a minimum each day): _____

_____

_____

_____

_____

_____

Contacts (calls/e-mails to people I need to connect with): _____

_____

_____

_____

_____

_____

_____

Habit (what am I working on this week, and how): _____

_____

_____

_____

_____

_____

_____

Notes, Ideas, and Inspirations (any ideas that came up during the morning ritual): _____

_____

_____

_____

_____

_____

_____

_____

_____

_____

_____

_____

_____

_____

_____

_____

_____

_____

_____

Evening Ritual for _____

Before you settle in for the night, sit comfortably with your journal in a quiet space—preferably one dedicated to your reflective and visualization work—and ask yourself the following empowering questions. Write down whatever comes up.

_____

_____

_____

_____

_____

_____

- Was I "on" and in the zone today or "off" and unbalanced?

_____

_____

_____

_____

_____

_____

_____

- What contributed to this feeling?

_____

_____

_____

_____

_____

_____

_____

- What were the top three positive things I accomplished or that happened today? What did I learn from them?

_____

_____

_____

_____

_____

- Are there unsolved challenges I would like my subconscious mind to help me solve tonight?

_____

_____

_____

_____

_____

_____

_____

- What went wrong today and what is the silver lining?

_____

_____

_____

_____

_____

Now enter a meditative state using Box Breathing, and then enter your mind gym in order to review your major goals and continue your ongoing visualization work. While in your mind gym, put any questions or problems that are bugging you to your counselor or to your subconscious. Pay attention to your dreams and any waking thoughts the next day—the answer will usually be there for you.

Morning Ritual for_____

When you awake in the morning, the first thing you will do is drink a large glass of fresh water, and then sit comfortably with your journal in a quiet space—preferably one dedicated to your reflective and visualization work—and ask yourself the following empowering questions. Write down whatever comes up.

- What and whom am I grateful for today?

_____

_____

_____

_____

_____

_____

_____

- What am I excited about and looking forward to doing today?

_____

_____

_____

_____

_____

_____

- What is my purpose, and do my plans for today connect me to it?

_____

_____

_____

_____

- How can I move the dial toward my goals today?

_____

_____

_____

_____

_____

_____

- To whom can I reach out and serve or thank today?

_____

_____

_____

_____

_____

- Are my goals still aligned with my purpose?

_____

_____

_____

_____

_____

_____

Next, spend a minimum of five minutes Box Breathing, then spend a minimum of five minutes in mindful movement (I do up to an hour some days). My preference is yoga, but tai chi, qi gong, or a short mindful walk will work. Finally, before you start your day, review your Daily or Weekly Focus Plan. Make any adjustments to ensure it's in alignment with the answers to your morning questions, and block time in your schedule for key project work or training.

Daily/Weekly Focus Plan for _____

The One Thing (the most important thing I will achieve this day and/
or week):

_____

_____

_____

_____

_____

Priority Tasks (that I must complete today or this week): _____

_____

_____

_____

_____

_____

Projects (to work on one step at a minimum each day): _____

_____

_____

_____

_____

_____

Contacts (calls/e-mails to people I need to connect with): _____

_____

_____

_____

_____

_____

_____

Habit (what am I working on this week, and how): _____

_____

_____

_____

_____

_____

_____

Notes, Ideas, and Inspirations (any ideas that came up during the
morning ritual): _____

Evening Ritual for _____

Before you settle in for the night, sit comfortably with your journal in a quiet space—preferably one dedicated to your reflective and visualization work—and ask yourself the following empowering questions. Write down whatever comes up.

_____

_____

_____

_____

_____

_____

- Was I "on" and in the zone today or "off" and unbalanced?

_____

_____

_____

_____

_____

_____

_____

- What contributed to this feeling?

_____

_____

_____

_____

_____

_____

_____

_____

- What were the top three positive things I accomplished or that happened today? What did I learn from them?

_____

_____

_____

_____

- Are there unsolved challenges I would like my subconscious mind to help me solve tonight?

_____

_____

_____

_____

_____

_____

- What went wrong today and what is the silver lining?

_____

_____

_____

_____

_____

Now enter a meditative state using Box Breathing, and then enter your mind gym in order to review your major goals and continue your ongoing visualization work. While in your mind gym, put any questions or problems that are bugging you to your counselor or to your subconscious. Pay attention to your dreams and any waking thoughts the next day—the answer will usually be there for you.

Morning Ritual for_____

When you awake in the morning, the first thing you will do is drink a large glass of fresh water, and then sit comfortably with your journal in a quiet space—preferably one dedicated to your reflective and visualization work—and ask yourself the following empowering questions. Write down whatever comes up.

- What and whom am I grateful for today?

_____

_____

_____

_____

_____

_____

_____

- What am I excited about and looking forward to doing today?

_____

_____

_____

_____

_____

_____

_____

- What is my purpose, and do my plans for today connect me to it?

_____

_____

_____

_____

- How can I move the dial toward my goals today?

_____

_____

_____

_____

_____

_____

- To whom can I reach out and serve or thank today?

_____

_____

_____

_____

_____

_____

- Are my goals still aligned with my purpose?

_____

_____

_____

_____

_____

_____

_____

Next, spend a minimum of five minutes Box Breathing, then spend a minimum of five minutes in mindful movement (I do up to an hour some days). My preference is yoga, but tai chi, qi gong, or a short mindful walk will work. Finally, before you start your day, review your Daily or Weekly Focus Plan. Make any adjustments to ensure it's in alignment with the answers to your morning questions, and block time in your schedule for key project work or training.

Daily/Weekly Focus Plan for _____

The One Thing (the most important thing I will achieve this day and/
or week):

_____

_____

_____

_____

_____

Priority Tasks (that I must complete today or this week): _____

_____

_____

_____

_____

_____

Projects (to work on one step at a minimum each day): _____

_____

_____

_____

_____

_____

Contacts (calls/e-mails to people I need to connect with): _____

_____

_____

_____

_____

_____

_____

Habit (what am I working on this week, and how): _____

_____

_____

_____

_____

_____

_____

Notes, Ideas, and Inspirations (any ideas that came up during the morning ritual): _____

_____

_____

_____

_____

_____

_____

_____

_____

_____

_____

_____

_____

_____

_____

_____

_____

_____

_____

Evening Ritual for _____

Before you settle in for the night, sit comfortably with your journal in a quiet space—preferably one dedicated to your reflective and visualization work—and ask yourself the following empowering questions. Write down whatever comes up.

_____

_____

_____

_____

_____

_____

• Was I "on" and in the zone today or "off" and unbalanced?

_____

_____

_____

_____

_____

_____

• What contributed to this feeling?

_____

_____

_____

_____

_____

_____

_____

- What were the top three positive things I accomplished or that happened today? What did I learn from them?

_____

_____

_____

_____

_____

- Are there unsolved challenges I would like my subconscious mind to help me solve tonight?

_____

_____

_____

_____

_____

_____

_____

- What went wrong today and what is the silver lining?

_____

_____

_____

_____

_____

_____

Now enter a meditative state using Box Breathing, and then enter your mind gym in order to review your major goals and continue your ongoing visualization work. While in your mind gym, put any questions or problems that are bugging you to your counselor or to your subconscious. Pay attention to your dreams and any waking thoughts the next day—the answer will usually be there for you.

Morning Ritual for_____

When you awake in the morning, the first thing you will do is drink a large glass of fresh water, and then sit comfortably with your journal in a quiet space—preferably one dedicated to your reflective and visualization work—and ask yourself the following empowering questions. Write down whatever comes up.

- What and whom am I grateful for today?

_____

_____

_____

_____

_____

_____

_____

- What am I excited about and looking forward to doing today?

_____

_____

_____

_____

_____

_____

- What is my purpose, and do my plans for today connect me to it?

_____

_____

_____

_____

• How can I move the dial toward my goals today?

_____

_____

_____

_____

_____

_____

• To whom can I reach out and serve or thank today?

_____

_____

_____

_____

_____

_____

• Are my goals still aligned with my purpose?

_____

_____

_____

_____

_____

_____

Next, spend a minimum of five minutes Box Breathing, then spend a minimum of five minutes in mindful movement (I do up to an hour some days). My preference is yoga, but tai chi, qi gong, or a short mindful walk will work. Finally, before you start your day, review your Daily or Weekly Focus Plan. Make any adjustments to ensure it's in alignment with the answers to your morning questions, and block time in your schedule for key project work or training.

Daily/Weekly Focus Plan for _____

The One Thing (the most important thing I will achieve this day and/or week):

_____

_____

_____

_____

_____

Priority Tasks (that I must complete today or this week): _____

_____

_____

_____

_____

_____

Projects (to work on one step at a minimum each day): _____

_____

_____

_____

_____

_____

Contacts (calls/e-mails to people I need to connect with): _____

_____

_____

_____

_____

_____

_____

Habit (what am I working on this week, and how): _____

_____

_____

_____

_____

_____

_____

Notes, Ideas, and Inspirations (any ideas that came up during the
morning ritual): _____

_____

_____

_____

_____

_____

_____

_____

_____

_____

_____

_____

_____

_____

_____

_____

_____

_____

Evening Ritual for _____

Before you settle in for the night, sit comfortably with your journal in a quiet space—preferably one dedicated to your reflective and visualization work—and ask yourself the following empowering questions. Write down whatever comes up.

_____

_____

_____

_____

_____

_____

- Was I "on" and in the zone today or "off" and unbalanced?

_____

_____

_____

_____

_____

_____

_____

- What contributed to this feeling?

_____

_____

_____

_____

_____

_____

_____

_____

• What were the top three positive things I accomplished or that happened today? What did I learn from them?

_____

_____

_____

_____

_____

• Are there unsolved challenges I would like my subconscious mind to help me solve tonight?

_____

_____

_____

_____

_____

_____

_____

• What went wrong today and what is the silver lining?

_____

_____

_____

_____

_____

_____

Now enter a meditative state using Box Breathing, and then enter your mind gym in order to review your major goals and continue your ongoing visualization work. While in your mind gym, put any questions or problems that are bugging you to your counselor or to your subconscious. Pay attention to your dreams and any waking thoughts the next day—the answer will usually be there for you.

Morning Ritual for_____

When you awake in the morning, the first thing you will do is drink
a large glass of fresh water, and then sit comfortably with your journal in a quiet space—preferably one dedicated to your reflective and
visualization work—and ask yourself the following empowering questions. Write down whatever comes up.

- What and whom am I grateful for today?

_____

_____

_____

_____

_____

_____

_____

- What am I excited about and looking forward to doing
  today?

_____

_____

_____

_____

_____

_____

_____

- What is my purpose, and do my plans for today connect
  me to it?

_____

_____

_____

_____

- How can I move the dial toward my goals today?

_____

_____

_____

_____

_____

_____

- To whom can I reach out and serve or thank today?

_____

_____

_____

_____

_____

_____

- Are my goals still aligned with my purpose?

_____

_____

_____

_____

_____

_____

Next, spend a minimum of five minutes Box Breathing, then spend a minimum of five minutes in mindful movement (I do up to an hour some days). My preference is yoga, but tai chi, qi gong, or a short mindful walk will work. Finally, before you start your day, review your Daily or Weekly Focus Plan. Make any adjustments to ensure it's in alignment with the answers to your morning questions, and block time in your schedule for key project work or training.

Daily/Weekly Focus Plan for _____

The One Thing (the most important thing I will achieve this day and/ or week):

_____

_____

_____

_____

_____

Priority Tasks (that I must complete today or this week): _____

_____

_____

_____

_____

_____

Projects (to work on one step at a minimum each day): _____

_____

_____

_____

_____

_____

Contacts (calls/e-mails to people I need to connect with): _____

_____

_____

_____

_____

_____

_____

Habit (what am I working on this week, and how): _____

_____

_____

_____

_____

_____

_____

Notes, Ideas, and Inspirations (any ideas that came up during the morning ritual): _____

_____

_____

_____

_____

_____

_____

_____

_____

_____

_____

_____

_____

_____

_____

_____

_____

_____

_____

Evening Ritual for _____

Before you settle in for the night, sit comfortably with your journal in a quiet space—preferably one dedicated to your reflective and visualization work—and ask yourself the following empowering questions. Write down whatever comes up.

_____

_____

_____

_____

_____

- Was I "on" and in the zone today or "off" and unbalanced?

_____

_____

_____

_____

_____

_____

- What contributed to this feeling?

_____

_____

_____

_____

_____

_____

_____

- What were the top three positive things I accomplished or that happened today? What did I learn from them?

_____

_____

_____

_____

_____

- Are there unsolved challenges I would like my subconscious mind to help me solve tonight?

_____

_____

_____

_____

_____

_____

_____

- What went wrong today and what is the silver lining?

_____

_____

_____

_____

_____

_____

Now enter a meditative state using Box Breathing, and then enter your mind gym in order to review your major goals and continue your ongoing visualization work. While in your mind gym, put any questions or problems that are bugging you to your counselor or to your subconscious. Pay attention to your dreams and any waking thoughts the next day—the answer will usually be there for you.

Morning Ritual for_____

When you awake in the morning, the first thing you will do is drink a large glass of fresh water, and then sit comfortably with your journal in a quiet space—preferably one dedicated to your reflective and visualization work—and ask yourself the following empowering questions. Write down whatever comes up.

- What and whom am I grateful for today?

_____

_____

_____

_____

_____

_____

_____

- What am I excited about and looking forward to doing today?

_____

_____

_____

_____

_____

_____

_____

- What is my purpose, and do my plans for today connect me to it?

_____

_____

_____

_____

• How can I move the dial toward my goals today?

_____

_____

_____

_____

_____

_____

• To whom can I reach out and serve or thank today?

_____

_____

_____

_____

_____

• Are my goals still aligned with my purpose?

_____

_____

_____

_____

_____

_____

Next, spend a minimum of five minutes Box Breathing, then spend a minimum of five minutes in mindful movement (I do up to an hour some days). My preference is yoga, but tai chi, qi gong, or a short mindful walk will work. Finally, before you start your day, review your Daily or Weekly Focus Plan. Make any adjustments to ensure it's in alignment with the answers to your morning questions, and block time in your schedule for key project work or training.

Daily/Weekly Focus Plan for _____

The One Thing (the most important thing I will achieve this day and/or week):

_____

_____

_____

_____

_____

Priority Tasks (that I must complete today or this week): _____

_____

_____

_____

_____

_____

Projects (to work on one step at a minimum each day): _____

_____

_____

_____

_____

_____

Contacts (calls/e-mails to people I need to connect with): _____

_____

_____

_____

_____

_____

_____

Habit (what am I working on this week, and how): _____

_____

_____

_____

_____

_____

_____

Notes, Ideas, and Inspirations (any ideas that came up during the
morning ritual): _____

_____

_____

_____

_____

_____

_____

_____

_____

_____

_____

_____

_____

_____

_____

_____

_____

_____

_____

_____

_____

Evening Ritual for _____

Before you settle in for the night, sit comfortably with your journal in a quiet space—preferably one dedicated to your reflective and visualization work—and ask yourself the following empowering questions. Write down whatever comes up.

_____

_____

_____

_____

_____

_____

- Was I "on" and in the zone today or "off" and unbalanced?

_____

_____

_____

_____

_____

_____

_____

- What contributed to this feeling?

_____

_____

_____

_____

_____

_____

_____

• What were the top three positive things I accomplished or that happened today? What did I learn from them?

_____

_____

_____

_____

_____

• Are there unsolved challenges I would like my subconscious mind to help me solve tonight?

_____

_____

_____

_____

_____

_____

_____

• What went wrong today and what is the silver lining?

_____

_____

_____

_____

_____

Now enter a meditative state using Box Breathing, and then enter your mind gym in order to review your major goals and continue your ongoing visualization work. While in your mind gym, put any questions or problems that are bugging you to your counselor or to your subconscious. Pay attention to your dreams and any waking thoughts the next day—the answer will usually be there for you.

Morning Ritual for_____

When you awake in the morning, the first thing you will do is drink a large glass of fresh water, and then sit comfortably with your journal in a quiet space—preferably one dedicated to your reflective and visualization work—and ask yourself the following empowering questions. Write down whatever comes up.

- What and whom am I grateful for today?

_____

_____

_____

_____

_____

_____

_____

- What am I excited about and looking forward to doing today?

_____

_____

_____

_____

_____

_____

_____

- What is my purpose, and do my plans for today connect me to it?

_____

_____

_____

_____

• How can I move the dial toward my goals today?

_____

_____

_____

_____

_____

_____

• To whom can I reach out and serve or thank today?

_____

_____

_____

_____

_____

• Are my goals still aligned with my purpose?

_____

_____

_____

_____

_____

_____

Next, spend a minimum of five minutes Box Breathing, then spend a minimum of five minutes in mindful movement (I do up to an hour some days). My preference is yoga, but tai chi, qi gong, or a short mindful walk will work. Finally, before you start your day, review your Daily or Weekly Focus Plan. Make any adjustments to ensure it's in alignment with the answers to your morning questions, and block time in your schedule for key project work or training.

Daily/Weekly Focus Plan for _____

The One Thing (the most important thing I will achieve this day and/or week):

_____

_____

_____

_____

_____

Priority Tasks (that I must complete today or this week): _____

_____

_____

_____

_____

_____

Projects (to work on one step at a minimum each day): _____

_____

_____

_____

_____

_____

Contacts (calls/e-mails to people I need to connect with): _____

_____

_____

_____

_____

_____

_____

Habit (what am I working on this week, and how): _____

_____

_____

_____

_____

_____

Notes, Ideas, and Inspirations (any ideas that came up during the morning ritual): _____

_____

_____

_____

_____

_____

_____

_____

_____

_____

_____

_____

_____

_____

_____

_____

Evening Ritual for _____

Before you settle in for the night, sit comfortably with your journal in
a quiet space—preferably one dedicated to your reflective and visualization work—and ask yourself the following empowering questions.
Write down whatever comes up.

_____

_____

_____

_____

_____

_____

• Was I "on" and in the zone today or "off" and unbalanced?

_____

_____

_____

_____

_____

_____

_____

• What contributed to this feeling?

_____

_____

_____

_____

_____

_____

_____

- What were the top three positive things I accomplished or that happened today? What did I learn from them?

_____

_____

_____

_____

_____

- Are there unsolved challenges I would like my subconscious mind to help me solve tonight?

_____

_____

_____

_____

_____

_____

_____

- What went wrong today and what is the silver lining?

_____

_____

_____

_____

_____

Now enter a meditative state using Box Breathing, and then enter your mind gym in order to review your major goals and continue your ongoing visualization work. While in your mind gym, put any questions or problems that are bugging you to your counselor or to your subconscious. Pay attention to your dreams and any waking thoughts the next day—the answer will usually be there for you.

Morning Ritual for_____

When you awake in the morning, the first thing you will do is drink a large glass of fresh water, and then sit comfortably with your journal in a quiet space—preferably one dedicated to your reflective and visualization work—and ask yourself the following empowering questions. Write down whatever comes up.

- What and whom am I grateful for today?

_____

_____

_____

_____

_____

_____

_____

- What am I excited about and looking forward to doing today?

_____

_____

_____

_____

_____

_____

- What is my purpose, and do my plans for today connect me to it?

_____

_____

_____

_____

• How can I move the dial toward my goals today?

_____

_____

_____

_____

_____

• To whom can I reach out and serve or thank today?

_____

_____

_____

_____

_____

• Are my goals still aligned with my purpose?

_____

_____

_____

_____

_____

_____

Next, spend a minimum of five minutes Box Breathing, then spend a minimum of five minutes in mindful movement (I do up to an hour some days). My preference is yoga, but tai chi, qi gong, or a short mindful walk will work. Finally, before you start your day, review your Daily or Weekly Focus Plan. Make any adjustments to ensure it's in alignment with the answers to your morning questions, and block time in your schedule for key project work or training.

Daily/Weekly Focus Plan for _____

The One Thing (the most important thing I will achieve this day and/
or week):

_____

_____

_____

_____

_____

Priority Tasks (that I must complete today or this week): _____

_____

_____

_____

_____

_____

Projects (to work on one step at a minimum each day): _____

_____

_____

_____

_____

_____

Contacts (calls/e-mails to people I need to connect with): _____

_____

_____

_____

_____

_____

_____

Habit (what am I working on this week, and how): _____

_____

_____

_____

_____

_____

_____

Notes, Ideas, and Inspirations (any ideas that came up during the
morning ritual): _____

_____

_____

_____

_____

_____

_____

_____

_____

_____

_____

_____

_____

_____

_____

_____

_____

_____

_____

Evening Ritual for _____

Before you settle in for the night, sit comfortably with your journal in a quiet space—preferably one dedicated to your reflective and visualization work—and ask yourself the following empowering questions. Write down whatever comes up.

_____

_____

_____

_____

_____

- Was I "on" and in the zone today or "off" and unbalanced?

_____

_____

_____

_____

_____

_____

_____

- What contributed to this feeling?

_____

_____

_____

_____

_____

_____

_____

_____

• What were the top three positive things I accomplished or that happened today? What did I learn from them?

_____

_____

_____

_____

_____

• Are there unsolved challenges I would like my subconscious mind to help me solve tonight?

_____

_____

_____

_____

_____

_____

_____

• What went wrong today and what is the silver lining?

_____

_____

_____

_____

_____

Now enter a meditative state using Box Breathing, and then enter your mind gym in order to review your major goals and continue your ongoing visualization work. While in your mind gym, put any questions or problems that are bugging you to your counselor or to your subconscious. Pay attention to your dreams and any waking thoughts the next day—the answer will usually be there for you.

Morning Ritual for_____

When you awake in the morning, the first thing you will do is drink a large glass of fresh water, and then sit comfortably with your journal in a quiet space—preferably one dedicated to your reflective and visualization work—and ask yourself the following empowering questions. Write down whatever comes up.

• What and whom am I grateful for today?

_____

_____

_____

_____

_____

_____

_____

• What am I excited about and looking forward to doing today?

_____

_____

_____

_____

_____

_____

_____

• What is my purpose, and do my plans for today connect me to it?

_____

_____

_____

_____

• How can I move the dial toward my goals today?

_____

_____

_____

_____

_____

_____

• To whom can I reach out and serve or thank today?

_____

_____

_____

_____

_____

_____

• Are my goals still aligned with my purpose?

_____

_____

_____

_____

_____

_____

Next, spend a minimum of five minutes Box Breathing, then spend a minimum of five minutes in mindful movement (I do up to an hour some days). My preference is yoga, but tai chi, qi gong, or a short mindful walk will work. Finally, before you start your day, review your Daily or Weekly Focus Plan. Make any adjustments to ensure it's in alignment with the answers to your morning questions, and block time in your schedule for key project work or training.

Daily/Weekly Focus Plan for _____

The One Thing (the most important thing I will achieve this day and/
or week):

_____

_____

_____

_____

_____

Priority Tasks (that I must complete today or this week): _____

_____

_____

_____

_____

_____

Projects (to work on one step at a minimum each day): _____

_____

_____

_____

_____

_____

Contacts (calls/e-mails to people I need to connect with): _____

_____

_____

_____

_____

_____

_____

Habit (what am I working on this week, and how): _____

_____

_____

_____

_____

_____

_____

Notes, Ideas, and Inspirations (any ideas that came up during the morning ritual): _____

_____

_____

_____

_____

_____

_____

_____

_____

_____

_____

_____

_____

_____

_____

_____

_____

_____

_____

_____

Evening Ritual for _____

Before you settle in for the night, sit comfortably with your journal in a quiet space—preferably one dedicated to your reflective and visualization work—and ask yourself the following empowering questions. Write down whatever comes up.

_____

_____

_____

_____

_____

_____

- Was I "on" and in the zone today or "off" and unbalanced?

_____

_____

_____

_____

_____

_____

_____

- What contributed to this feeling?

_____

_____

_____

_____

_____

_____

_____

_____

• What were the top three positive things I accomplished or that happened today? What did I learn from them?

_____

_____

_____

_____

_____

• Are there unsolved challenges I would like my subconscious mind to help me solve tonight?

_____

_____

_____

_____

_____

_____

_____

• What went wrong today and what is the silver lining?

_____

_____

_____

_____

_____

_____

Now enter a meditative state using Box Breathing, and then enter your mind gym in order to review your major goals and continue your ongoing visualization work. While in your mind gym, put any questions or problems that are bugging you to your counselor or to your subconscious. Pay attention to your dreams and any waking thoughts the next day—the answer will usually be there for you.

Morning Ritual for_____

When you awake in the morning, the first thing you will do is drink a large glass of fresh water, and then sit comfortably with your journal in a quiet space—preferably one dedicated to your reflective and visualization work—and ask yourself the following empowering questions. Write down whatever comes up.

• What and whom am I grateful for today?

_____

_____

_____

_____

_____

_____

_____

• What am I excited about and looking forward to doing today?

_____

_____

_____

_____

_____

_____

_____

• What is my purpose, and do my plans for today connect me to it?

_____

_____

_____

_____

• How can I move the dial toward my goals today?

_____

_____

_____

_____

_____

_____

• To whom can I reach out and serve or thank today?

_____

_____

_____

_____

_____

_____

• Are my goals still aligned with my purpose?

_____

_____

_____

_____

_____

_____

Next, spend a minimum of five minutes Box Breathing, then spend a minimum of five minutes in mindful movement (I do up to an hour some days). My preference is yoga, but tai chi, qi gong, or a short mindful walk will work. Finally, before you start your day, review your Daily or Weekly Focus Plan. Make any adjustments to ensure it's in alignment with the answers to your morning questions, and block time in your schedule for key project work or training.

Daily/Weekly Focus Plan for _____

The One Thing (the most important thing I will achieve this day and/
or week):

_____

_____

_____

_____

_____

Priority Tasks (that I must complete today or this week): _____

_____

_____

_____

_____

_____

Projects (to work on one step at a minimum each day): _____

_____

_____

_____

_____

_____

Contacts (calls/e-mails to people I need to connect with): _____

_____

_____

_____

_____

_____

_____

Habit (what am I working on this week, and how): _____

_____

_____

_____

_____

_____

_____

Notes, Ideas, and Inspirations (any ideas that came up during the morning ritual): _____

_____

_____

_____

_____

_____

_____

_____

_____

_____

_____

_____

_____

_____

_____

_____

_____

_____

Evening Ritual for _____

Before you settle in for the night, sit comfortably with your journal in a quiet space—preferably one dedicated to your reflective and visualization work—and ask yourself the following empowering questions. Write down whatever comes up.

_____

_____

_____

_____

_____

_____

- Was I "on" and in the zone today or "off" and unbalanced?

_____

_____

_____

_____

_____

_____

_____

- What contributed to this feeling?

_____

_____

_____

_____

_____

_____

_____

- What were the top three positive things I accomplished or that happened today? What did I learn from them?

_____

_____

_____

_____

- Are there unsolved challenges I would like my subconscious mind to help me solve tonight?

_____

_____

_____

_____

_____

_____

- What went wrong today and what is the silver lining?

_____

_____

_____

_____

_____

Now enter a meditative state using Box Breathing, and then enter your mind gym in order to review your major goals and continue your ongoing visualization work. While in your mind gym, put any questions or problems that are bugging you to your counselor or to your subconscious. Pay attention to your dreams and any waking thoughts the next day—the answer will usually be there for you.

Morning Ritual for_____

When you awake in the morning, the first thing you will do is drink a large glass of fresh water, and then sit comfortably with your journal in a quiet space—preferably one dedicated to your reflective and visualization work—and ask yourself the following empowering questions. Write down whatever comes up.

- What and whom am I grateful for today?

_____

_____

_____

_____

_____

_____

_____

- What am I excited about and looking forward to doing today?

_____

_____

_____

_____

_____

_____

- What is my purpose, and do my plans for today connect me to it?

_____

_____

_____

_____

- How can I move the dial toward my goals today?

_____

_____

_____

_____

_____

_____

- To whom can I reach out and serve or thank today?

_____

_____

_____

_____

_____

_____

- Are my goals still aligned with my purpose?

_____

_____

_____

_____

_____

_____

Next, spend a minimum of five minutes Box Breathing, then spend a minimum of five minutes in mindful movement (I do up to an hour some days). My preference is yoga, but tai chi, qi gong, or a short mindful walk will work. Finally, before you start your day, review your Daily or Weekly Focus Plan. Make any adjustments to ensure it's in alignment with the answers to your morning questions, and block time in your schedule for key project work or training.

Daily/Weekly Focus Plan for _____

The One Thing (the most important thing I will achieve this day and/
or week):

_____

_____

_____

_____

_____

Priority Tasks (that I must complete today or this week): _____

_____

_____

_____

_____

_____

Projects (to work on one step at a minimum each day): _____

_____

_____

_____

_____

_____

Contacts (calls/e-mails to people I need to connect with): _____

_____

_____

_____

_____

_____

_____

Habit (what am I working on this week, and how): _____

_____

_____

_____

_____

_____

_____

Notes, Ideas, and Inspirations (any ideas that came up during the
morning ritual): _____

_____

_____

_____

_____

_____

_____

_____

_____

_____

_____

_____

_____

_____

_____

_____

_____

_____

_____

Evening Ritual for _____

Before you settle in for the night, sit comfortably with your journal in a quiet space—preferably one dedicated to your reflective and visualization work—and ask yourself the following empowering questions. Write down whatever comes up.

_____

_____

_____

_____

_____

_____

- Was I "on" and in the zone today or "off" and unbalanced?

_____

_____

_____

_____

_____

_____

_____

- What contributed to this feeling?

_____

_____

_____

_____

_____

_____

_____

_____

- What were the top three positive things I accomplished or that happened today? What did I learn from them?

_____

_____

_____

_____

_____

- Are there unsolved challenges I would like my subconscious mind to help me solve tonight?

_____

_____

_____

_____

_____

_____

_____

_____

- What went wrong today and what is the silver lining?

_____

_____

_____

_____

_____

Now enter a meditative state using Box Breathing, and then enter your mind gym in order to review your major goals and continue your ongoing visualization work. While in your mind gym, put any questions or problems that are bugging you to your counselor or to your subconscious. Pay attention to your dreams and any waking thoughts the next day—the answer will usually be there for you.

Pre-Event Ritual

Use this ritual when facing a major mission, race, or challenge and you simply must be at your peak. Once habituated, this can be a five-minute exercise with a powerful impact on your performance.

First, as you approach the time of the event (depending upon the duration and difficulty of the event, this can be days, hours, or minutes before go-time), take action to avoid external distractions (some events, like a race or workout, have a known start time; others are not as known, but this principle applies in either situation). So find a quiet space where you can be alone, perhaps sitting in the car or in a separate room. If you are in a crowded area, just sit and close your eyes and people will leave you alone. Don't worry about what others think about you—they're likely jealous that you have the courage to take care of yourself instead of engaging in the common nervous pre-event chitchat.

Next, perform a "dirt-dive" visualization to size up your performance in the event and size down your enemy. The enemy can be an actual opponent, other competitors, or even your board of directors! In this visualization, see yourself dominating the situation, totally in control, and see your competitor as capitulating, congratulating you, or weak and ineffective—whatever is appropriate for your situation. Focus on your physiology and psychology during each stage of the event as you see it unfold in your mind. Perform deep breathing during this dirt-dive. This sets the stage for the rest of the ritual.

Next review your goals and strategy for the mission or challenge. See yourself accomplishing these with ease. Double-check your strategy against the reality of the moment: Is it KISS? Are there any last-minute modifications you need to make? Is there a way to make it even simpler? Are you prepared for the unknown with contingency plans?

Finally, initiate an internal dialogue with a powerful mantra to maintain a positive mind-set, speech, posture, and state of being as you finish your pre-event ritual and launch into performing.

Pre-Event Ritual

Use this ritual when facing a major mission, race, or challenge and you simply must be at your peak. Once habituated, this can be a five-minute exercise with a powerful impact on your performance.

First, as you approach the time of the event (depending upon the duration and difficulty of the event, this can be days, hours, or minutes before go-time), take action to avoid external distractions (some events, like a race or workout, have a known start time; others are not as known, but this principle applies in either situation). So find a quiet space where you can be alone, perhaps sitting in the car or in a separate room. If you are in a crowded area, just sit and close your eyes and people will leave you alone. Don't worry about what others think about you—they're likely jealous that you have the courage to take care of yourself instead of engaging in the common nervous pre-event chitchat.

Next, perform a "dirt-dive" visualization to size up your performance in the event and size down your enemy. The enemy can be an actual opponent, other competitors, or even your board of directors! In this visualization, see yourself dominating the situation, totally in control, and see your competitor as capitulating, congratulating you, or weak and ineffective—whatever is appropriate for your situation. Focus on your physiology and psychology during each stage of the event as you see it unfold in your mind. Perform deep breathing during this dirt-dive. This sets the stage for the rest of the ritual.

Next review your goals and strategy for the mission or challenge. See yourself accomplishing these with ease. Double-check your strategy against the reality of the moment: Is it KISS? Are there any last-minute modifications you need to make? Is there a way to make it even simpler? Are you prepared for the unknown with contingency plans?

Finally, initiate an internal dialogue with a powerful mantra to maintain a positive mind-set, speech, posture, and state of being as you finish your pre-event ritual and launch into performing.

Pre-Event Ritual

Use this ritual when facing a major mission, race, or challenge and you simply must be at your peak. Once habituated, this can be a five-minute exercise with a powerful impact on your performance.

First, as you approach the time of the event (depending upon the duration and difficulty of the event, this can be days, hours, or minutes before go-time), take action to avoid external distractions (some events, like a race or workout, have a known start time; others are not as known, but this principle applies in either situation). So find a quiet space where you can be alone, perhaps sitting in the car or in a separate room. If you are in a crowded area, just sit and close your eyes and people will leave you alone. Don't worry about what others think about you—they're likely jealous that you have the courage to take care of yourself instead of engaging in the common nervous pre-event chitchat.

Next, perform a "dirt-dive" visualization to size up your performance in the event and size down your enemy. The enemy can be an actual opponent, other competitors, or even your board of directors! In this visualization, see yourself dominating the situation, totally in control, and see your competitor as capitulating, congratulating you, or weak and ineffective—whatever is appropriate for your situation. Focus on your physiology and psychology during each stage of the event as you see it unfold in your mind. Perform deep breathing during this dirt-dive. This sets the stage for the rest of the ritual.

Next review your goals and strategy for the mission or challenge. See yourself accomplishing these with ease. Double-check your strategy against the reality of the moment: Is it KISS? Are there any last-minute modifications you need to make? Is there a way to make it even simpler? Are you prepared for the unknown with contingency plans?

Finally, initiate an internal dialogue with a powerful mantra to maintain a positive mind-set, speech, posture, and state of being as you finish your pre-event ritual and launch into performing.

Post-Event Ritual

Begin with the "Finding the Silver Lining" exercise on page 57. When you've completed that, you'll want to redirect your attention to a new mission or challenge and reengage your planning and training. This will be an iterative process, but it can be started in this post-event ritual with some ideas jotted down about what's next. This post-event course correction can reveal a lot of interesting things. What if you voluntarily took a challenge like an Iron Man race, but you really did not enjoy the process or the event? Would you do another Iron Man just because you can? I wouldn't waste major chunks of life training for something I didn't enjoy the first time! What is another goal or 20X challenge you can set instead?

For a business venture, it may be that your first shot was off the mark. Would you try the same thing again, and if so, how would you adjust your approach? Most entrepreneurial ventures take three or more shots to find the product or revenue model that gets the gears to click. Reframing, reflecting, and redirecting your efforts will help you stay on purpose and moving on the right goals. Ensure that in this process you also reconnect with your "why" and get squarely behind the new goal to reenergize yourself so you can hit it hard when you get back to the playing field the next day.

_____

_____

_____

_____

_____

_____

_____

_____

_____

Post-Event Ritual

Begin with the "Finding the Silver Lining" exercise on page 57. When you've completed that, you'll want to redirect your attention to a new mission or challenge and reengage your planning and training. This will be an iterative process, but it can be started in this post-event ritual with some ideas jotted down about what's next. This post-event course correction can reveal a lot of interesting things. What if you voluntarily took a challenge like an Iron Man race, but you really did not enjoy the process or the event? Would you do another Iron Man just because you can? I wouldn't waste major chunks of life training for something I didn't enjoy the first time! What is another goal or 20X challenge you can set instead?

For a business venture, it may be that your first shot was off the mark. Would you try the same thing again, and if so, how would you adjust your approach? Most entrepreneurial ventures take three or more shots to find the product or revenue model that gets the gears to click. Reframing, reflecting, and redirecting your efforts will help you stay on purpose and moving on the right goals. Ensure that in this process you also reconnect with your "why" and get squarely behind the new goal to reenergize yourself so you can hit it hard when you get back to the playing field the next day.

_____

_____

_____

_____

_____

_____

_____

_____

_____

Post-Event Ritual

Begin with the "Finding the Silver Lining" exercise on page 57. When you've completed that, you'll want to redirect your attention to a new mission or challenge and reengage your planning and training. This will be an iterative process, but it can be started in this post-event ritual with some ideas jotted down about what's next. This post-event course correction can reveal a lot of interesting things. What if you voluntarily took a challenge like an Iron Man race, but you really did not enjoy the process or the event? Would you do another Iron Man just because you can? I wouldn't waste major chunks of life training for something I didn't enjoy the first time! What is another goal or 20X challenge you can set instead?

For a business venture, it may be that your first shot was off the mark. Would you try the same thing again, and if so, how would you adjust your approach? Most entrepreneurial ventures take three or more shots to find the product or revenue model that gets the gears to click. Reframing, reflecting, and redirecting your efforts will help you stay on purpose and moving on the right goals. Ensure that in this process you also reconnect with your "why" and get squarely behind the new goal to reenergize yourself so you can hit it hard when you get back to the playing field the next day.

_____

_____

_____

_____

_____

_____

_____

Quarterly Focus Plan for _____

The One Thing (the most important thing I will achieve this quarter):

_____

_____

_____

_____

Top 3 Targets for the Quarter: _____

_____

_____

_____

_____

_____

_____

Top 3 Tasks for Each Target: _____

_____

_____

_____

_____

_____

_____

Top Contacts to Make: _____

_____

_____

_____

_____

_____

_____

New Habit to Integrate: _____

_____

_____

_____

_____

_____

_____

Notes, New Ideas, and Inspirations: _____

_____

_____

_____

_____

_____

_____

_____

_____

_____

_____

_____

_____

_____

_____

_____

_____

_____

Quarterly Focus Plan for _____

The One Thing (the most important thing I will achieve this quarter):

_____

_____

_____

_____

Top 3 Targets for the Quarter: _____

_____

_____

_____

_____

_____

Top 3 Tasks for Each Target: _____

_____

_____

_____

_____

_____

Top Contacts to Make: _____

_____

_____

_____

_____

_____

_____

New Habit to Integrate: _____

_____

_____

_____

_____

_____

_____

Notes, New Ideas, and Inspirations: _____

_____

_____

_____

_____

_____

_____

_____

_____

_____

_____

_____

_____

_____

_____

_____

_____

_____

_____

Quarterly Focus Plan for _____

The One Thing (the most important thing I will achieve this quarter):

_____

_____

_____

_____

Top 3 Targets for the Quarter: _____

_____

_____

_____

_____

_____

_____

Top 3 Tasks for Each Target: _____

_____

_____

_____

_____

_____

_____

Top Contacts to Make: _____

_____

_____

_____

_____

_____

_____

New Habit to Integrate: _____

_____

_____

_____

_____

_____

Notes, New Ideas, and Inspirations: _____

_____

_____

_____

_____

_____

_____

_____

_____

_____

_____

_____

_____

_____

_____

_____

Quarterly Focus Plan for _____

The One Thing (the most important thing I will achieve this quarter):

_____

_____

_____

_____

Top 3 Targets for the Quarter: _____

_____

_____

_____

_____

_____

Top 3 Tasks for Each Target: _____

_____

_____

_____

_____

_____

Top Contacts to Make: _____

_____

_____

_____

_____

_____

_____

New Habit to Integrate: _____

_____

_____

_____

_____

_____

_____

Notes, New Ideas, and Inspirations: _____

_____

_____

_____

_____

_____

_____

_____

_____

_____

_____

_____

_____

_____

_____

_____

_____

_____

_____

_____

Quarterly Focus Plan for _____

The One Thing (the most important thing I will achieve this quarter):

_____

_____

_____

_____

Top 3 Targets for the Quarter: _____

_____

_____

_____

_____

_____

_____

Top 3 Tasks for Each Target: _____

_____

_____

_____

_____

_____

_____

Top Contacts to Make: _____

_____

_____

_____

_____

_____

_____

New Habit to Integrate: _____

_____

_____

_____

_____

_____

_____

Notes, New Ideas, and Inspirations: _____

_____

_____

_____

_____

_____

_____

_____

_____

_____

_____

_____

_____

_____

_____

_____

_____

_____

Quarterly Focus Plan for _____

The One Thing (the most important thing I will achieve this quarter):

_____

_____

_____

_____

Top 3 Targets for the Quarter: _____

_____

_____

_____

_____

_____

Top 3 Tasks for Each Target: _____

_____

_____

_____

_____

_____

Top Contacts to Make: _____

_____

_____

_____

_____

_____

New Habit to Integrate: _____

_____

_____

_____

_____

_____

_____

Notes, New Ideas, and Inspirations: _____

_____

_____

_____

_____

_____

_____

_____

_____

_____

_____

_____

_____

_____

_____

_____

_____

_____

_____

Quarterly Focus Plan for _____

The One Thing (the most important thing I will achieve this quarter):

_____

_____

_____

_____

Top 3 Targets for the Quarter: _____

_____

_____

_____

_____

_____

Top 3 Tasks for Each Target: _____

_____

_____

_____

_____

_____

Top Contacts to Make: _____

_____

_____

_____

_____

_____

New Habit to Integrate: _____

_____

_____

_____

_____

_____

_____

Notes, New Ideas, and Inspirations: _____

_____

_____

_____

_____

_____

_____

_____

_____

_____

_____

_____

_____

_____

_____

_____

_____

_____

_____

_____

_____

_____

Quarterly Focus Plan for _____

The One Thing (the most important thing I will achieve this quarter):

_____

_____

_____

_____

Top 3 Targets for the Quarter: _____

_____

_____

_____

_____

_____

Top 3 Tasks for Each Target: _____

_____

_____

_____

_____

_____

Top Contacts to Make: _____

_____

_____

_____

_____

_____

New Habit to Integrate: _____

_____

_____

_____

_____

_____

_____

Notes, New Ideas, and Inspirations: _____

_____

_____

_____

_____

_____

_____

_____

_____

_____

_____

_____

_____

_____

_____

_____

_____

_____

_____

Quarterly Focus Plan for _____

The One Thing (the most important thing I will achieve this quarter):

_____

_____

_____

_____

Top 3 Targets for the Quarter: _____

_____

_____

_____

_____

_____

Top 3 Tasks for Each Target: _____

_____

_____

_____

_____

_____

Top Contacts to Make: _____

_____

_____

_____

_____

_____

New Habit to Integrate: _____

_____

_____

_____

_____

_____

_____

Notes, New Ideas, and Inspirations: _____

_____

_____

_____

_____

_____

_____

_____

_____

_____

_____

_____

_____

_____

_____

_____

_____

_____

Quarterly Focus Plan for _____

The One Thing (the most important thing I will achieve this quarter):

_____

_____

_____

_____

Top 3 Targets for the Quarter: _____

_____

_____

_____

_____

_____

Top 3 Tasks for Each Target: _____

_____

_____

_____

_____

_____

Top Contacts to Make: _____

_____

_____

_____

_____

_____

New Habit to Integrate: _____

_____

_____

_____

_____

_____

_____

Notes, New Ideas, and Inspirations: _____

_____

_____

_____

_____

_____

_____

_____

_____

_____

_____

_____

_____

_____

_____

_____

_____

_____

_____

_____

Quarterly Focus Plan for _____

The One Thing (the most important thing I will achieve this quarter):

_____

_____

_____

_____

Top 3 Targets for the Quarter: _____

_____

_____

_____

_____

_____

_____

Top 3 Tasks for Each Target: _____

_____

_____

_____

_____

_____

_____

Top Contacts to Make: _____

_____

_____

_____

_____

_____

_____

New Habit to Integrate: _____

_____

_____

_____

_____

_____

Notes, New Ideas, and Inspirations: _____

_____

_____

_____

_____

_____

_____

_____

_____

_____

_____

_____

_____

_____

_____

_____

_____

Quarterly Focus Plan for _____

The One Thing (the most important thing I will achieve this quarter):

_____

_____

_____

_____

Top 3 Targets for the Quarter: _____

_____

_____

_____

_____

_____

Top 3 Tasks for Each Target: _____

_____

_____

_____

_____

_____

_____

Top Contacts to Make: _____

_____

_____

_____

_____

_____

_____

New Habit to Integrate: _____

_____

_____

_____

_____

_____

_____

Notes, New Ideas, and Inspirations: _____

_____

_____

_____

_____

_____

_____

_____

_____

_____

_____

_____

_____

_____

_____

_____

_____

_____

_____

Annual Focus Plan for _____

Purpose/Vision for My Life (carry forward and adjust as it evolves):

_____

_____

_____

_____

_____

_____

_____

Vision for My Business or Work Role (carry forward and adjust as it evolves): _____

_____

_____

_____

_____

_____

_____

_____

Top 6 Values (and what I can do this year to get closer to them): _

_____

_____

_____

_____

_____

_____

_____

Top 3 Mission Goals for My Life (carry forward and adjust as they evolve):_____

_____

_____

_____

_____

_____

_____

_____

Top 3 Mission Goals for the Next 3 Years (carry forward and adjust as they evolve): _____

_____

_____

_____

_____

_____

_____

Top 3 Targets for This Year: _____

_____

_____

_____

_____

_____

_____

_____

Must-Dos for Reaching My Top 3 Targets: _____

_____

_____

_____

_____

_____

_____

_____

Top 20 Contacts to Make: _____

_____

_____

_____

_____

_____

_____

_____

_____

_____

New Habit to Integrate: _____

_____

_____

_____

_____

_____

_____

Notes, Ideas, and Inspirations (have/be/do list): _____

_____

_____

_____

_____

_____

_____

_____

_____

_____

_____

_____

_____

_____

_____

_____

_____

_____

_____

_____

_____

_____

_____

_____

_____

_____

_____

_____

_____

_____

Annual Focus Plan for _____

Purpose/Vision for My Life (carry forward and adjust as it evolves):

_____

_____

_____

_____

_____

_____

_____

Vision for My Business or Work Role (carry forward and adjust as it
evolves): _____

_____

_____

_____

_____

_____

_____

_____

Top 6 Values (and what I can do this year to get closer to them): _

_____

_____

_____

_____

_____

_____

_____

Top 3 Mission Goals for My Life (carry forward and adjust as they evolve):_____

_____

_____

_____

_____

_____

_____

Top 3 Mission Goals for the Next 3 Years (carry forward and adjust as they evolve): _____

_____

_____

_____

_____

_____

_____

Top 3 Targets for This Year: _____

_____

_____

_____

_____

_____

_____

Must-Dos for Reaching My Top 3 Targets: _____

_____

_____

_____

_____

_____

_____

_____

Top 20 Contacts to Make: _____

_____

_____

_____

_____

_____

_____

_____

_____

_____

New Habit to Integrate: _____

_____

_____

_____

_____

_____

_____

Notes, Ideas, and Inspirations (have/be/do list): _____

_____

_____

_____

_____

_____

_____

_____

_____

_____

_____

_____

_____

_____

_____

_____

_____

_____

_____

_____

_____

_____

_____

_____

_____

_____

_____

_____

_____

_____

Annual Focus Plan for _____

Purpose/Vision for My Life (carry forward and adjust as it evolves):

_____

_____

_____

_____

_____

_____

_____

Vision for My Business or Work Role (carry forward and adjust as it evolves): _____

_____

_____

_____

_____

_____

_____

_____

Top 6 Values (and what I can do this year to get closer to them): _

_____

_____

_____

_____

_____

_____

_____

Top 3 Mission Goals for My Life (carry forward and adjust as they evolve):_____

_____

_____

_____

_____

_____

_____

Top 3 Mission Goals for the Next 3 Years (carry forward and adjust as they evolve): _____

_____

_____

_____

_____

_____

_____

Top 3 Targets for This Year: _____

_____

_____

_____

_____

_____

_____

_____

Must-Dos for Reaching My Top 3 Targets: _____

_____

_____

_____

_____

_____

_____

_____

_____

Top 20 Contacts to Make: _____

_____

_____

_____

_____

_____

_____

_____

_____

_____

New Habit to Integrate: _____

_____

_____

_____

_____

_____

_____

_____

Notes, Ideas, and Inspirations (have/be/do list): _____

_____

_____

_____

_____

_____

_____

_____

_____

_____

_____

_____

_____

_____

_____

_____

_____

_____

_____

_____

_____

_____

_____

_____

_____

_____

_____

Weekly Training Plan

Time	Monday	Tuesday	Wednesday

Thursday	Friday	Saturday	Sunday

Weekly Training Plan

Time	Monday	Tuesday	Wednesday

Thursday	Friday	Saturday	Sunday

Weekly Training Plan

Time	Monday	Tuesday	Wednesday

Thursday	Friday	Saturday	Sunday

REFLECTIONS AND INSIGHTS_____

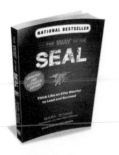